QUANTUM
CREATIVITY

QUANTUM CREATIVITY

Nine Principles

to Transform the Way You Work

PAMELA MEYER

CB

CONTEMPORARY BOOKS

Library of Congress Cataloging-in-Publication Data

Meyer, Pamela.
    Quantum creativity : nine principles to transform the way you work /
Pamela Meyer.
       p.   cm.
    A revised version of the Chicago, Ill. : YeZand Press © 1997 edition.
    Includes bibliographical references.
    ISBN 0-8092-2439-9
    1. Creative thinking.   2. Work—Psychological aspects.   I. Title.
BF408.M465   2000
153.3'5—dc21   99-57946
                                               CIP

Quotation on p. vii courtesy of Dee Hock.

Excerpt on p. 109 from *A Simpler Way*, by Margaret Wheatley and Myron Kellner-Rogers (San Francisco: Berrett-Koehler, 1996). Copyright © 1996 by Margaret Wheatley and Myron Kellner-Rogers. Reprinted with permission of the publisher. All rights reserved. 1-800-929-2929.

Excerpts on pp. 19 and 128 from *Bird by Bird*, by Anne Lamott (New York: Pantheon Press, 1994). Copyright © 1994, Anne Lamott. Reprinted by permission of the publisher.

Excerpt on p. 88 from "Thoughts on Theatre: An Interview with John Glover and Cherry Jones," *Equity News*, September 1995. Copyright © 1995, Equity News, New York. Reprinted by permission of the publisher.

Excerpt on p. 30 from *The Universe Is a Green Dragon*, by Brian Swimme (Santa Fe: Bear & Co., 1984). Copyright © 1984, Bear & Co.

Excerpt on p. 64 from *Truth in Comedy*, by Charna Halpern, Del Close, and Kim "Howard" Johnson (Colorado Springs: Meriweather Publishing, 1993). Copyright © 1993, Meriweather Publishing.

Excerpt on pp. 52–53 from "Toward a Process for Critical Response," by Liz Lerman. Originally appeared in *Alternate Roots*, a publication of the Regional Organization of Theatres South, summer 1993. Copyright © 1993.

Excerpts on pp. 91 and 125 from *Letters to a Young Poet*, by Rainer Maria Rilke, translated by M. D. Herter Norton. Translation copyright 1934, 1954 by W. W. Norton & Company, Inc., renewed © 1962, 1982 by M. D. Herter Norton. Reprinted by permission of W. W. Norton & Company.

Excerpts on pp. 64, 73–74, 107, and 172 reprinted from *Fast Company* magazine. All rights reserved. To subscribe, please call (800) 688-1545.

Cover and interior design by Monica Baziuk
Back-cover photograph by Isabel Raci

Published by Contemporary Books
A division of NTC/Contemporary Publishing Group, Inc.
4255 West Touhy Avenue, Lincolnwood (Chicago), Illinois 60712-1975 U.S.A.
Copyright © 2000 by Pamela Meyer
Printed in the United States of America
International Standard Book Number: 0-8092-2439-9
00 01 02 03 04 05 ML 19 18 17 16 15 14 13 12 11 10 9 8 7 6 5 4 3 2

TO THE CREATIVITY,
COURAGE,
AND LIGHT OF
RACHEL MEYER

We are at that very point in time when a four-hundred-year-old age is rattling in its deathbed and another is struggling to be born—a shift of culture, science, society, and institutions enormously greater than the world has ever experienced. Ahead, the possibility of the regeneration of individuality, liberty, community, and ethics such as the world has never known, and a harmony with nature, with one another, and with the divine intelligence such as the world has ever dreamed.

—Dee Hock, Founder of Visa

Contents

Acknowledgements

I owe much of the inspiration for this book to my students and clients who test-drove these concepts again and again over the years and encouraged me to spread the word. Many of these adventurous souls generously shared their stories to bring this book to life. Thanks to my many cheerleaders, readers, and advisers, among them Donald McKay, Ph.D., Patricia Monaghan, Ph.D., Mary Cross, Michael Hammermeister, my colleagues at DePaul University, Sarah Bradley, Maria Baseleon, Ellen Credille, Izzy Gesell, Mari Pat Varga, the "Lab Rats," Holly Shulman, and Deborah Jackson. Big love to my mother, Rachel Meyer, the biggest cheerleader of all.

How wonderful it was to have such a collaborator and champion in my agent, Andrea Pedolsky, and such enthusiasm and support from my editor, Kara Leverte. More thanks still to Craig Bolt and all the other pros at NTC/Contemporary.

Introduction

Technology has given many of us equal access to information and to lightning-fast communication. As we begin the twenty-first century on a relatively level playing field, your ability to be flexible, listen, communicate, collaborate, and respond quickly and creatively will make more difference in your success and satisfaction than any amount of data or technology. Creativity is the core competency for this millennium. And not just any kind of creativity, not just adding new twists to existing products and services, but Quantum Creativity—creativity that manifests the truly unexpected by transcending what has been done before.

In these pages you will read stories from people at Lucent Technologies, PricewaterhouseCoopers, American Airlines, Automatic Data Processing, and many others I have enjoyed working with over the years, who actively develop their creativity competency. Each engages in the process of transformation: transforming the *way* they work as the work itself transforms.

In all of my years consulting and speaking, I have never worked with an organization, business, association, or corporation. Rather, I have worked with thousands of individuals with dynamic lives, secret passions, and untapped creative potentials. Yes, these individuals work for larger organizations, serve on teams, and work to fulfill missions, visions, and quarterly quotas. And, when it comes to transforming the way they work, they have started at the beginning—with themselves.

This is good news and bad news: the bad news is the problem is us. The *good* news is the problem is us. This is where hope lies. Individuals transform more easily than do institutions. Thus, this book was not written for your board of directors, company, department, or team, nor even for your CEO, supervisor, team leader, or coworker. It was written for you. It was written with hope in mind.

To fulfill the promise of Quantum Creativity, you will find yourself challenged to transform the way you work, to do things differently. Children transform boxes into spaceships, and sheets and furniture into elaborate forts by doing things differently. Improvisers create entire evenings of theater by doing things differently. Administrators, lab assistants, flight attendants, data processors, salespeople, and many others have industry-changing breakthroughs by doing things differently. Scientists reframe their assumptions about the laws of physics and open the door for giant leaps in technology by doing things differently. Managers simultaneously improve quality and performance and increase employee job satisfaction by doing things differently.

What do all of these innovative acts have in common? Each is propelled by the enthusiastic flow of energy into action, action filled with wide-eyed possibility. This creative energy is available to all, though few access it. To find your way to this infinite resource you need to transform the way you work and release yourself from the stifling beliefs that have limited your creative acts. Doing things differently does not imply doing for different's sake, but means changing the way most of us work. We are quite good at doing—too good, in fact. We are so busy doing that we miss our quiet inspirations, the subtle voices and serendipitous connections in our everyday experience—these insights are available to us from *being*, not doing.

Being opens the door to awareness and presence, the conditions necessary for creativity. Creativity requires a lively awareness of possibilities. Most of our doing is devoid of this awareness, and thereby misses many opportunities and innovations. There are legendary examples of "accidents" that spawned innovations because someone was present with a lively awareness of possibilities: Post-it Notes, aspartame sweetener, and Scotchgard fabric protector are only a few examples. Heightened consciousness is the first step toward a new kind of action. Most likely your workday demands that you re-act quickly to whatever your environment offers up— new information, changing organizational structures, market fluctuations, and all of the unexpected events of the day. Re-action tends to draw from superficial resources, limited by past experience, the way it has been done before, and outdated information. Re-action spawns re-creation, rather than original thought or behavior, which necessarily springs from our origin, our deeper center. Originality represents a significant shift in the way most of us work.

Before I expand on the concept of Quantum Creativity, I want to develop working definitions for two words you will see throughout the book: *creativity* and *innovation*. While these words have often been used interchangeably, for our purposes it is important to make a distinction. Creativity is a way of being—a state necessary for the act of creation, for bringing forth the new and original. Though creativity does not always lead to innovation, it is the foundation for it. Innovation is applied or directed creativity—an idea, product, service, or procedure that is both new and useful. Creativity is the process; innovation is the outcome.

Transformation thrives in the process; creativity thrives in transformation. While you will read many examples of innovation emerging from creativity, the intention is to illuminate the conditions from which innovation emerges—the state of being that led to the doing. Though difficult to quantify, richness, quality, satisfaction, engagement, and delight are just a few characteristics of this dynamic state. Through the nine principles of Quantum Creativity you will rediscover your limitless creativity. You will transform the way you work. Even better, you will enjoy your own transformation and unfoldment along the way.

This book is about the entire process of living a creative life, a life of infinite possibilities. Work is not a subset of life. Separating business from the rest of life sets up the very limiting boxes that stifle creative expression. I am not suggesting that you take your work home with you, but that you find a new integrity, integrating your values, passion, and vision into all of your life's endeavors. It is all too easy to tolerate limited possibilities in one area of life under the illusion that such a disability will not have a larger impact: "It's OK if I don't express my creativity at work, I do that at home with the kids," or, "My work demands every ounce of my passion, I don't have any left over at the end of the day."

Work may look very different from one person to the next. For some, it takes place in an office during traditional business hours; for others it has little formal structure, yet is fully engaging nonetheless. For most of us work is an expression of our identity. It offers a mother lode of possibilities. Robin Sheerer, author of *No More Blue Mondays*, writes, "Work provides a focus for our lives, grants us an identity, and is the single greatest arena available to us for self-expression, contribution, and personal growth." It is no wonder that we will feel the impact throughout our lives and relationships if we are not in alignment with our passion and creative potential when we are at work. Work can be a source of great pain and great satisfaction. So the primary purpose of this book is to help you transform the way you work and expand creativity in your business, and that will not happen for you if you insist on removing your work experience from the rest of your life. Creativity cannot flourish this way.

Because a creative life is a process and defies the confines of boxes and lines, you will find examples and inspiration here for enlivening your awareness of possibilities in many of life's dimensions. These examples are not intended to be a how-to guide for increasing creativity. There is no single prescription to cure what ails us; such an idea is itself mechanistic in nature. We can learn much, however, from those who have gone before us. Their courage and wisdom inspire us as we find our own paths.

In search of this new integrity, you will find stories and examples from both the traditional and nontraditional worlds of work. A parent will discover a new way to motivate his children, an executive will discover a new strategy for decision-making, a theater director will discover how to trust collaborative creativity, a quality supervisor will discover how to tap into his team's innovation resources—all by integrating the desire for a more rewarding work experience with personal values, operating principles, and behavior.

But how can we find this integrity when very early in life so many of us are socialized *out* of our lively awareness and a healthy relationship to creativity, play, and wonder? In grade school we were taught that having (or appearing to have) the "right" answer, fitting in, and getting peer approval were more important than trusting our own instincts. We learned that answers were more important than questions, so we eventually stopped asking them altogether. We started doubting our ideas, second-guessing our passions, and eventually, stagnating in a world of limited options.

There is hope. It is possible to reignite your natural curiosity and to restore yourself to a lively awareness of possibilities. You can break free from the beliefs that have barred you from realizing your potential. You have all of the resources to live a rich life, full of wonder and possibilities. Your resources and the road to rediscovering them are yours alone. Just as no one can define another's spiritual experience, neither can another tell you how to experience your creativity. While flexibility, discovery, insight, and surprise-ability are all reflections of creativity, there is no one right way to achieve or experience them. This book is not intended to define a specific experience for you—that would be arrogant and disrespectful. Rather, it will serve as a map to lead you back to what you once spontaneously and intuitively knew.

Quantum Creativity will free you from limiting perceptions of yourself and your business's possibilities. Perceived limits are illusions, and yet they can have a powerful impact on reality and on the decisions you make each day. If you believe you can only sell your product or service to existing clients, and that you can expect x percent of repeat business, then that is the reality you will likely manifest. If you perceive (with lively awareness), however, that the market has not even begun to be tapped and that the possibilities are unlimited, then that will be your experience.

Here is the paradox: in order to expand creative possibility we must move beyond limiting beliefs, yet we all necessarily function *within* a set of beliefs (e.g., you may believe that commitment and perseverance lead to success, or that most people are honest, or that family is paramount). Your challenge is not to throw out all worldviews or to be without boundaries or belief systems of any kind (an unrealistic and mythical prerequisite for creativity), but to distinguish between those that are useful and those that have narrowed your awareness of possibilities.

Physicists in the late 1800s and early 1900s experienced just such a break from limiting perceptions as they studied the behavior of subatomic particles. Newton's laws of mechanics, the reliance on certainty, and objective observation quickly proved useless in understanding the subatomic world. Quantum theory, spawned by these early explorations, made possible some of our most significant scientific advances, including lasers, computers, and microwaves. The irony is inspiring: the most innovative breakthroughs in science challenged the limits of the scientific model itself.

Quantum physics reminds us, by analogy, of the essential nature of creativity. Creative life energy is filled with possibility; we cannot "observe" creativity without participating in it, nor can we experience it without changing it or ourselves. There are no objective observers, only participants who channel and transform creative energy. In fact, our expectations and beliefs about our creativity may well determine how that creativity manifests.

Quantum physics teaches that we cannot observe something without changing it. No longer can we separate our world from our experience of the world. No longer can we compartmentalize, cordon off, or isolate. We cannot do it for rewarding personal relationships. We cannot do it for successful businesses. Quantum Creativity offers a solution and an invitation—one rich with participation, collaboration, and even delight.

Creative expression is limited only by your ability to experience yourself and your world. Realizing your full potential has more to do with *getting out of the way* and allowing what is already there to reveal itself, than with learning anything new. The lessons from quantum physics are profound: the universe is fundamentally holistic, participatory, observer-created, and based in potential energy. What fertile ground for creativity! *Quantum* Creativity, therefore, is a lively state of being that fosters transformation and cocreation of infinite possibilities.

A note on the analogy: comparing processes in physics to processes in creativity illuminates the matter, helping you see the challenges and potential of creativity in a new light. Breathe easy—you do not need to have a science degree to understand the connection. I draw on common principles rather than complex mathematical equations. And, like all analogies, the comparison will eventually break down. Before it does, my hope is that you will have an expanded awareness of the mystery and possibilities of your own creativity.

Improvisation is used as both an analogy, as in "see how your work life is like or can be like a theatrical improvisation," and as a verb describing what your work can be, as in "Sarah and Juan improvised with the time and resources available to find an innovative solution." Drawing insights from such diverging fields as physics and improvisation may seem odd. There is, however, a compelling connection: transformation. Improvisation is the art of transformation. Players transform and are transformed as they cocreate new realities on stage. Likewise, the observer in physics transforms that which she observes, fostering a new term, *participant/observer*. The stories of transformation in nature and in creative collaboration may well inspire your own transformation. They may help you discover and develop your transform-ability.

| YOUR INVITATION |

This book invites you to bring your whole self to work—to turn every challenge and every interaction into a creative collaboration. Each of the following chapters presents one of the nine principles to support you in expanding your vision. Each principle invites you to make a quantum shift in perception that will allow you to become aware of and unleash the lively possibilities in your life.

After the chapter's principle is presented, you will read about the Learned Blocks that may have kept you from a lively experience of possibilities. Some will fit you to a T, while others may appear irrelevant to your experience. Apply what is useful to you—no need wasting your energy trying to squeeze into something that doesn't fit. While you cannot be taught creativity, you *can* identify the blocks. Acknowledging these blocks is the first step toward moving beyond them. It is the first step toward Doing Things Differently— the third section of each chapter.

This third section gives examples and ideas for practicing each principle. A person in a darkened room has little chance to create light by sitting in the dark and pondering the reasons for the darkness, the ramifications of continued darkness, and the impact darkness has had on his or her life. You, too, will fail to rediscover life's possibilities if you lose yourself in pondering and analyzing similar questions about creativity. The person in the darkened room simply needs to get up and turn on the light (or light a candle, or pull back the blinds, or turn on a flashlight). You simply need to do things differently to remove the darkness of creative blocks and illuminate your potential.

The nine Quantum Creativity principles have a holographic nature; just as each fragment of a hologram plate contains the information of the entire image, so do many of the principles of Quantum Creativity contain the wisdom of the whole. While the principles are, by necessity, presented in a linear fashion, they are nonlinear in nature. Sometimes it is useful to follow them in the order I have set down, and at other times you may follow another order altogether. More often than not, they take on a life of their own based on the present moment. Call them up as you need them. Live them, challenge them, explore them.

Maharishi Mahesh Yogi, one of my spiritual teachers, challenged his students not to believe anything he said until they found it to be true for themselves. He encouraged skepticism *with* participation. After all, how can we find out if something is true for us if we don't try it for ourselves? Personal growth is a rigorous process—a participatory one. It is not simply an intellectual experience, but one that is also physical, emotional, and spiritual.

---

1. Sheerer, XI.

QUANTUM CREATIVITY

Rick Walters had enjoyed a successful career at the New Jersey corporate headquarters of Automatic Data Processing (ADP). He had worked his way up to a position of authority and respect and had built an impressive track record over the years. Comfortable and successful, why did he say yes when the offer came to relocate to the Chicago office, to move from his prestigious staff role to a field management position? Why did he choose to give up some nice perks and incentives? Why did he choose to leave the known and leap into the unknown?

"I just knew it was the right thing to do. I accepted the offer before I even knew all of the details. I call it my 'gut check.' It's something you just have to go with." The "right thing" it was! Today, as division vice president and general manager, Rick has grown professionally and personally while leading ADP to even greater heights with his fresh vision. His wisdom extends to his management staff, "I've noticed that what puts my managers over the edge from being good to being great, is their ability to perform their own 'gut checks.' Those that only think about the monetary impact of their decisions are shortsighted."

LISTEN TO YOUR ESSENCE

Tap the Power of Intuition and Silence

| **THE PRINCIPLE** | *Listen to Your Essence* is your opportunity to move from shortsighted to *in*-sighted. Rick Walters, along with a growing number of executives, understands that without insight there can be no true vision. Seeing and acting in the lightning-paced, high-tech world requires depth of perception for success.

In this chapter you will learn to listen with depth, receptivity, willingness, acceptance, and availability. This may be a bit uncomfortable for you action-oriented, goal-obsessed, outcome based, bottom-line driven folks. Yet listen you must, if you are to access the infinite potential of your creative energy. You must become comfortable with stillness before you can be effective in action. Your stillness will inform your action in ways your intellect and past experience never dreamed possible.

Most artists admit that they first needed to learn to receive before they could communicate through their medium. Visual artists and photographers learn to see before they can create; musicians learn to hear before they can play; dancers and actors learn to feel before they can perform. Visionaries in all fields of business and art spend more time listening than talking.

The Gap Between the Known and the Unknown

Jonas Salk asserted, after years of observing his own and others' research breakthroughs, that creativity depends on the dynamic interaction between intuition and reason. We make decisions every day based on the interplay of intuition and reason—decisions based on inadequate facts.[1] We choose employees, prioritize our day's "action items," select furnishings and marketing strategy—all using a lively mix of facts and feeling.

The gap between the known and the unknown provides an almost magnetic field—a dynamic void where the unexpected and truly innovative can be zapped into life. Striking the balance between the known and unknown allows us to tap this universal power. Unfortunately, we have been schooled to rely solely on the known and verifiable, reducing the information we receive from our Essence into material for the next cocktail party: "I was this close to getting on that flight to Phoenix when something told me to call my office. They had been trying to find me to tell me the meeting was canceled!"

As I wrote in the Introduction, creativity demands a lively awareness of possibilities. Awareness first; action second. Do not shortchange yourself of a full panoramic view of the landscape. Listening may reveal a mountain of opportunity or a volcano of volatility, signaling you to defer action, gather more information, or turn back altogether. Missing either will have significant consequences later on.

Listen to Your Essence is a direct challenge to mechanistic perception. In a world conceived as a machine, Essence, intuition, hunches, and gut feelings have little value. Only empirical evidence, quantifiable results, and verifiable facts are worthy of attention, appropriate fodder for decision-making and problem-solving.

Action based only on data will be missing your integrity. Listen to your essence and you will also hear the heartbeat of your moral center. It may not come to you in words, but in a sensation or disease signaling you to reconsider. While the numbers may point you toward taking that new job, signing that contract, or closing that deal, your Essence may tell you it does not add up. Are you willing to trust this less-than-certain information, when the facts support you in action?

In the quantum world, scientists (who stake their careers on verifiable documentation) have had to accept a level of uncertainty—to enlarge the scientific model, grounded in numbers and exact measurements, and to include contradiction, paradox, and probability. The challenge of the quantum worldview is to accept that there are things we simply cannot know through direct observation (such as the simultaneous speed and location of an electron). We must transcend the world of the tangible and concrete to a deeper, perhaps more universal, source. This demands integration of mind, body, and spirit.

In this integrity, you may receive information in any number of ways, through any number of channels. Some say *how* you receive information is dictated by your neurophysiology; others say it's by socialization or a combination of both. You may "listen" to a quiet inner voice, to a vision, or a physical sensation. Most people learn to listen to what comes most consistently—the channel coming in clearest on their "Essential Broadcasting Network."

Even the staunchest skeptics of this less tangible source of information would have to acknowledge some wisdom in listening to what is "absolutely necessary and important," a dictionary definition of *essential*. Would you not relish a business day when you were only served up the "absolutely necessary and important" information? Listen, and you will get just the information you need.

This past year I received early and unsolicited interest in this book you are reading from a handful of small publishers. One was brazen enough to send me a contract after only a brief phone conversation. Another also wanted to move quickly, but thankfully the negotiation process hit some speedbumps as we discussed specific details. My initial excitement ("Somebody wants to buy my book!") was soon overshadowed by a queasy feeling in my gut. "Sloooooow down," it told me. "Explore your options. Do this right."

So I slowed down. First, using my professional network, I found the right agent to represent the book. Then she put me through my paces writing a new proposal. Oddly, the extra work did not put me off; it reinforced that I had made the right decision. Once the proposal was ready for prime time, my agent did excellent work finding just the right publisher. Almost nine months after my Essence told me to slow down, I had a solid offer on the table. All was right with the world. This time, I did not feel queasy at the prospect of a commitment, but felt elated as I signed the contracts.

The more expert you are in your field, the more resistant you may be to listening. My relative innocence to the publishing industry may have given me enough humility to trust my discomfort. You, however, may have worked in your field for years, backed up by more years of formal and informal education. You read the daily business papers and journals. You track relevant stocks and monitor trends. You attend all of the important conferences and conventions. You even hire expensive consultants to help you implement cutting-edge processes and systems. You invest a significant amount of time each year gathering information. And this information serves you well. It helps you make hundreds of decisions, large and small, each week.

Yet you are only using a portion of your creative resources if data is your only source of decision-making criteria. Quantum Creativity reveals itself *within* the gap between the known and unknown. Here true transformation is possible. You must make some space for quantum leap to occur. Remember, you are forming the conditions for the unexpected, not the linear and predictable ideas of the causal world. Like the electron that simply ceases to exist in one energy state and reappears in another, your creative impulses will appear out of your lively Essence. Settle in and spend some time. Get comfortable in your own gap, your own unknown.

The stakes extend beyond your work life. Quantum Creativity happily invades all areas of your life. If you choose to ignore your inner life, to not "know thyself," you may be in for great distress. Dr. Rachel Naomi Remen, medical director and cofounder of Commonwealth Cancer Help Program, and assistant clinical professor at University of California, says:

> It is possible to talk to someone who has chosen carefully every sofa cushion, every pair of stockings and every lipstick and yet who still does not have a sense of the meaning of her life. If we could pay that same kind of attention to our inner world, we would come a lot closer to living well.

Ignoring information delivered from the "inner world" is documented to have serious impact on physical health. When information (intuitive "hits," emotional unease, physical distress) is denied, the body internalizes it and eventually manifests it as disease. Medical intuitive Caroline Myss says, "Your biography is your biology." In other words, if you don't pay attention to the information the first time around, you will most certainly have to deal with it when it manifests as illness.

This pattern has a macroscopic translation in business. Executives, managers, and leaders re-create the same cycle when they deny their deeper wisdom. Ed, a colleague, recently endured a lengthy legal and criminal investigation of his office manager, Bea. For years, he had a nagging feeling that all was not right with the business accounts despite best information to the contrary. In addition to the empirical evidence, his family had enjoyed getting to know Bea's family. This familiarity seemed grounds for trust and made it easier to dismiss his occasional misgivings. Until one early morning, while taking a walk, it struck him like a lightening bolt, "Bea is stealing from me!" This time he couldn't ignore it.

Ed flew into action, telling Bea to take the week off, sealing the office, and hiring an outside accounting firm to review the books with a fine-tooth comb. Within days his Essential information was confirmed. Bea had been doctoring the books and skimming from client deposits for five years to the tune of more that $300,000. Ouch. Now Ed pays attention when he gets a nagging feeling.

It's true that *Listen to Your Essence* can keep you out of harm's way, but that is not enough for success in business today. Constant innovation, discovery, and exploration are necessary. Quantum Creativity relies on a steady stream of Essential information. An internal study by Frank Carrubba, then head of HP Labs (now executive VP of Product Technology at Philips Electronics) found the biggest distinction between successful product development teams and the truly extraordinary "out of the box" teams was not a higher level of talent, motivation, or vision, as might be expected. It was a higher level of authenticity and caring. He said, "The people on these breakthrough teams found in themselves a quality of truth, and brought it out in everyone, so that no one had to pretend to be something that they weren't."

Authenticity and Origin

Authenticity is a deep connection to our origin. *Originality*, a word often mentioned in the same breath as *creativity*, connotes that which is novel, or different from the status quo. When you allow yourself to listen, you cannot help but be original. After all, no one can listen to *your* Essence, nor you to theirs. What comes to you springs from your origin, and is expressed through your wonderful thoughts, images, language, and emotion. No other human being or techno-gizmo can replace that.

Remember the last time you fell in love? Was it the data, empirical evidence, and information that compelled you? Or something that transcended anything you could perceive with your senses? When you fall in love, what do you fall in love with? You are drawn to the core, nontransitory and completely original. If this Essence is compelling enough to fall in love (the most generous, life-affirming of human emotions) with in another, is it not compelling enough to listen to in yourself?

Some of us, out of personal doubt or misplaced authority, discover we have stepped out of our authenticity and integrity (and thereby, our originality). Such disintegration severely limits creative potential. In my first months of business consulting and speaking I was nervous that my years working in professional theater would negatively impact my credibility. So I tried to re-create myself in the image of my clients through dress, language, and behavior. In other words, I attempted to abandon my own truth, my origin, to serve their needs. Luckily, I was miserable at my masquerade and quickly realized I was being hired precisely because I *didn't* look, talk, or behave according to my clients' expectations. They hired me to learn what artists know about creativity and collaboration. They wanted to learn how to take advantage of new information at a moment's notice; how to lead in the workplace and marketplace without fear of taking risks; how to thrive in a climate of constant change. How could I be of any use if I tried to communicate through a veil of deception? I couldn't. You can't either.

Leadership today must be grounded in personal truth. Charles Handy, professor at the London Business School, writes, "Integrity comes naturally if you live for your vision. In other words, the vision cannot be something thought up in the drawing office. To be real, it has to come from the deepest parts of you. . . ."[2]

Before we can lead with our authenticity and inspire it in others, before we can listen to our Essence, we must know this core, which is essentially us and perhaps, essentially universal, exists. Some describe it as intuition or an inner voice, while others experience it spiritually, naming it higher power or God.

Here are a few of my favorite descriptions of this source:

Intuition occurs when we directly perceive facts outside the range of the usual five senses and independently of any reasoning process.[3]

> —Mona Lisa Schulz, M.D., Ph.D.
> Author, *Awakening Intuition*

Essence is [an] internal deep voice of wisdom. It is an internal compass that gives us direction. It is extremely important to have a strong and constant relationship with our Essence in order not to lose sight of who we are.

> —Jeff Tworek, Salesperson

I call it my "gut check." It just feels obvious.

> —Rick Walters
> Vice President, ADP

Essence is mostly spiritual. It is an inner voice that guides me when I ask it to. I also think that my Essence is stronger in my sleep and comes through during my dreams. Sometimes if I go to bed thinking of a problem, I dream about it and wake up with an answer.

> —Lori Doll
> Former student

Eureka!

> —Archimedes

Perhaps these descriptions remind you that you know more about your Essence than you thought. Language always limits us when describing the mysterious, illusive, or spiritual. Any words we try to put to that which is essentially us, and yet much greater than us, limits the limitless. Only because the form of this book is necessarily one of language must I find words to communicate that which is essentially unnamable. I refer to the experience primarily as "Essence" and occasionally as "intuition" or "higher power." I do not intend for these words to define any single experience, but to communicate the *possibilities* of experience.

Getting Out of the Way

Some believe that Essence or a higher power must be mystical and sensational, something very unlike day-to-day experiences. This dramatization of spirituality can cut us off from what is right in front of us, from what we already know. Medical intuitive, M.D. and Ph.D, Mona Lisa Schulz says that not only is intuition not mystical, it is something we all share, "Intuition is just another sense, like seeing or feeling or hearing. . . . We are all intuitive."[4]

We do not need to work at being spiritual; we are striving for something that is already there. In the same way, we do not need to work at being creative. We *are* creative beings. We came into the world this way. To listen is to let go of what cuts us off from a clear, consistent relationship with our creative spirit; it is "getting out of the way."

When we have difficulty getting out of the way, it's possible that we have forgotten the true nature of listening. Most of us think we are good listeners, although, more often than not, when we think we are listening, we are busy with our own thoughts and composing responses. We are being busy talking (usually in our heads) when we should be listening. I have often heard people describe prayer as asking for help, and meditation as listening for the answer. Many of us forget the listening part.

In my communication and collaboration workshops, I start by teaching listening skills. Listening serves as the foundation for all types of communication—even communication with ourselves. If we are not available to clearly receive incoming information, we certainly cannot make good use of the information we do hear. Inaccurate or distorted information is useless at best and dangerous at worst. We begin relationships that aren't right for us, take unrewarding jobs, and make purchases we later regret, all because we are unwilling or unable to practice *Listen to Your Essence*.

When we first practice listening, it is not unusual to hear nothing or to experience only the chatter of our frenetic thoughts: "My elbow itches . . . I think I've put on a few pounds this month . . . wonder if I chose the right health plan . . . was the card I sent for Mother's Day too sappy. . . . " And we're off! Have faith. Building a relationship with your Essence is a process, and, like all relationships, it needs regular attention to grow.

Inspiration

The subatomic world has an Essential counterpart. Electrons may occupy only certain levels of energy. Electrons naturally go into the lowest available energy level, or state of least excitation, but the lowest energy levels can accommodate the fewest electrons, so some electrons must occupy higher energy levels.[5] In the same way, we, too, gravitate toward our Essence when we allow ourselves to be without distraction. Our ground state is the source of infinite power and creative potential.

The more we know about the world of subatomic particles, the more we see Essence reflected therein. Most of the volume of the atom is empty (matter is concentrated in the nucleus) and subatomic particles behave as both waves and particles. In quantum field theory the field from which these particle-wave-energy impulses spring (and to which they return) is considered anything but empty—at least not in the way we have come to think of emptiness. It is a dynamic field, a field of all possibilities, a field of infinite creative potential. The essence of matter has the same range of possibilities as the essence of our being, the essence of our creative spirit. All too often we miss this connection because we have been taught to think of mind and matter as separate.

Inspired by this analogy, we cannot separate our physical selves and our creative processes from our Essence. A mechanistic culture encourages us to dismember body from spirit. For centuries Eastern philosophers have called this separation an illusion. The death of our creative self is brought on by living this illusion. The tangible, that which we can verify with our five senses, has power over the intangible, the *extra*-sensory. Unfortunately, like relying on only one news source, we may only get one side of the story. Quantum Creativity asks that you round the edges and eliminate the sides, compartments, and dark corners. Emancipate yourself from the bonds of symmetrical, cause-and-effect thinking. After all, we call it *in*spiration, not *out*spiration.

When we allow ourselves the time and space to experience the essential level of our being, we are often surprised at how much we do know. Like the dynamic quantum field, our Essence is anything but empty. It is the source of all our thoughts, intuitions, and passions—of infinite energy and possibilities.

Theatrical improvisers tap into this rich source for moment-to-moment inspiration, as they channel their Essence directly into live performance. Stage improvisation contains all of the elements of your workday: pressure to think on your feet, unexpected collaborative opportunities, and the bottom-line need to produce. The only difference is that stage improvisers have a keen awareness of their challenges and have a heightened pressure to produce in front of a live audience. Understanding the roots of improvisation may give you renewed appreciation for your creative gifts.

Theatrical improvisation has been traced to ancient shamanic traditions. The shaman, or spiritual elder, of a tribe entered a trance and gave his or her body over as a "theater for the gods."[6] The experience was transformative for both shaman and congregation, although the shaman often had no conscious memory of what transpired. Jesters, poets, and actors later became secular counterparts to the shaman by channeling a deep creative spirit for audiences to share.[7] Many an actor has described feeling as if their feet never touched the ground, or having little memory of the details, after a particularly inspired performance.

In the United States, the late Viola Spolin is considered the mother of contemporary theatrical improvisation. Inspired by her teacher, Neva Boyd, she developed a series of games for children as part of a Works Progress Administration (WPA) program in the thirties. She later expanded these games for use in the classroom and for training actors. Spolin's son, Paul Sills, grew up with these games and, as a student at the University of Chicago in the late forties and early fifties, used them to develop topical original work with his company, The Compass Players, which later spawned Second City in 1959.[8] Second City continues as a major force in the training of actors and a model for *Saturday Night Live* and traditional and experimental improvisation troupes.

In all of its manifestations, the improvisational impulse is constant. Throughout the ages improvisation has taught people to "respond to the immediate stimuli of the environment,"[9] and its early roots in spiritual traditions remain important today. To respond to the "immediate stimuli of the environment," we let go of the logic and control that often keeps us stuck and prevents us from noticing the subtle impulses of our Essence. Many of us are comfortable listening to and living in accordance with our linear, rational left brain. Improvisation requires us to let go of rational understanding and practicality. It compels us to respond out of intuition and trust.

Artists, parents, teachers, and healers, like improvisers, have long relied on a connection with Essence to meet the moment-to-moment challenges in their work. They start with a plan or a vision, and know that they need to be willing to throw that plan out at any moment in response to a new discovery. Those unavailable to their Essence struggle to keep their plans intact or to maintain illusions of control for control's sake, rather than honor the mischievous, unpredictable creative process that is life.

As this chapter's opening story confirms, intuition has emerged from the arts, mysticism, and what once was considered the proprietary domain of women. This Essential wisdom plays a significant role in everything from new product development to hiring decisions. Sherman Stratford studied companies such as AT&T, Pepsi Co, and Aetna that now offer introspection and reflection training to their management executives. Edward McCraken, CEO of Silicon Graphics says, "The most important trait of a good leader is knowing who you are. In our industry very often we don't have time to think. You have to do all your homework, but then you have to go with your intuition without letting your mind get in the way."[10]

Practicing the principle of "listen to your essence" can reveal a wealth of information, whether it is the hunch we follow in business, or a clearer understanding of our values, defining principles, and purpose. Unfortunately, the riches of our Essence are not always readily available to us, because along the way we have picked up a few learned blocks.

| LEARNED BLOCKS |

Learned blocks are the powerful messages that cut us off from seeing life's possibilities. Insidious and often unconscious, the worldview we construct out of these myths is solid, but not invincible. Once we identify these blocks, we can let go of them and do things differently.

Second-Guessing Intuition

We learned to second-guess intuition. We mistrust anything that is not concrete, practical, or verifiable. Whether we sit on an idea in a problem-solving session at work without sharing it, or go against our better judgment by doing something contrary to our gut wisdom, we devalue the messages of our Essence.

We all have stories of things going badly when we didn't trust our intuition. Rick Walters at ADP didn't come to his current wisdom by accident. Like most of us, he can look back with twenty-twenty vision on the impact of decisions based solely on data. "We were in a somewhat volatile period and at risk of losing some of our top performers. We felt we should do something in terms of the compensation package. We were right on the edge, but didn't. We let the budget rule our choice. The decision paid off poorly in retention of key associates—a classic case of being penny-wise and pound-foolish"

Agenda

Sometimes your own agenda (a predecided course of action) cuts you off from hearing the deeper wisdom. You may have such unbridled excitement about your new business venture (relationship, upcoming vacation), that you don't avail yourself of any information that might contradict your rigid agenda. You see, when you have an agenda, you can rationalize anything. If you have not already earned some war wounds from this learned block, you will. Or, you can avoid the pain altogether by noticing a red flag when you find yourself unwilling to hear information contrary to your plan.

I came close to jeopardizing my business by not seeing one such big red flag flapping in my face. I mistook it for a warm summer breeze. My company had produced a product that was getting positive responses from my clients and was beginning to find a wider audience. It seemed a perfect time to leverage the momentum, by engaging a professional to help get the word out and line up appropriate press coverage.

My excitement led me to interview a number of professionals with solid track records. I checked their references; I ran the numbers; I visualized the possibilities; I borrowed the money (a lot of money); I signed a contract. I did not seriously consider alternatives. (After all, hiring a professional was the next step; anyone in my position would do the same thing—"But, Mom, all the *other* kids are doing it!") I did not stop and check in with myself, get quiet, get all the facts—I did not listen.

I mistook my urgency ("If I don't do this now, I'll miss the opportunity!") for good, clear information. I didn't question where it came from, like the kid who so badly wants a new baseball mitt for his birthday that he doesn't question where his playground friend got the over-generous gift. Need I say that my investment did not pay off, causing me great financial and emotional distress? In fact, it is I who was stuck paying off the investment two years after the contract expired.

Authorities

Try as we might to do the right thing, sometimes we even get in trouble when we listen to authorities. There is nothing inherently wrong with listening to authorities. It is one way to find guidance when we face challenges in our lives. It becomes a block when we give our power away to these authorities without checking in with our Essence, the ultimate authority. We get caught up in the "shoulds" of society or expectations of peers and family, just like the townspeople who oohed and aahed as the emperor proudly walked naked down the street in his "new clothes." It becomes more important to meet the expectations of authorities than to risk rocking the boat by following the wisdom of our Essence.

Most of the amenities we take for granted today would never have found their way into production if the idea originator(s) had allowed this block to stifle their enthusiasm and cloud their vision.

Paul Dickson chronicles a number of examples in his "Future File": "Thomas Edison, legendary for his championship of exploration, proclaimed the limits of electricity for home use, 'Just as certain as death, [George] Westinghouse will kill a customer within six months after he puts in a system of any size.'" Authorities in their respective fields have made similar cryptic pronouncements on automobiles, air travel, television, radio, The Beatles, and PCs. So where does that leave us? Back at our own authority.

Busyness

It takes some of us longer than others to start listening, because we are caught up in busyness. We tell ourselves that we're too busy for creativity. Busyness is the drug of choice for many—and why not? There are so many things to do: clear off our desk, learn that new software package, prepare for the afternoon meeting, meet with a client, and call the vet to schedule a dental appointment for the dog. Before we know it, we don't even need to bother with those nasty nagging feelings.

Les has worked in social services most of his life. Each day presents hundreds of opportunities to focus on other people's needs and on innumerable projects:

> *I found that I was spending so much time focusing outside of myself, that when I needed to know what I was feeling, I couldn't. There are other times when I know I was using my busyness to avoid things I just didn't want to deal with. I still do sometimes. It's a hard habit to break.*

How many times have well-meaning friends advised us to "just keep busy" when we experience difficult periods in our lives? Next time you are tempted to fly into action, ask yourself whether you are in business or in busyness. You cannot be in busyness and have vision, or have balance and room for the playful dance of the known and unknown, for mystery and surprise. Busyness is an effective way to numb feelings. Feelings, nonetheless, are the lifeline back to your Essence. When you cut that line, it's hard to find your way back.

Unfortunately, you can get used to this disconnection and not hear the news flashes from your Essence when you need them most. Poet Addrienne Rich is less politic than I. She calls us to task for emotional dishonesty, saying, "The liar in her terror wants to fill up the void, with anything. Her lies are a denial of her fear; a way of maintaining control."[11] "Liar?" This may be the wake-up call for you to start doing things differently.

| DOING THINGS DIFFERENTLY |

Transforming the way you work is not accomplished through intellectual understanding alone, but by also doing things differently. The following are a few ideas.

H.A.L.T.

It is sometimes impossible to imagine simplicity in the rush of your day. Deadlines can feel like working while double-parked; the clock is always ticking. If it is not ticking on your immediate challenges, then it is on the larger ones—the imaginary timelines you set for your professional and personal assent. Whoa! Hold up a minute! H.A.L.T.! (I have shamelessly borrowed this acronym from the twelve-step tradition. It is a perfect antidote to busyness.) Stop right there. Don't make another move.

Do this especially if you are *H*ungry, *A*ngry, *L*onely, or *T*ired (I add Sick to my list). I have learned, through years of hard-won experience, that I do not make good decisions in any of these altered states, let alone make a connection with Essence. HALT! Stop right there and eat, feel, socialize, sleep, and get well. Take care of these most pressing needs before you even think of going deeper. Go ahead, go home, and take a nap. We'll wait for you.

Stand and Wait

"They also serve who only stand and wait."[12] Milton's familiar line reminds us of the value of doing nothing or what *appears* to be nothing. Yogis who spend much of their lives in meditation, and monks and others who take vows of silence teach us the value of taking time to listen—of simply being for the sake of being. I have often wondered if these gentle, unassuming souls are the ones who truly keep the world from spinning off its axis, instead of the movers and shakers to whom we give so much credit in Western culture.

Acquire the habit of listening, even when you don't think you need the input. Be like the CEO who leaves her door open, thereby announcing her availability to have people stop in, share new information, and air concerns. She knows that every time she opens the door she will not be flooded with a line of employees eager to provide new insights, and by establishing the routine of an open door these insights will come when they are ready.

You can establish the same open-door policy with your Essence, your source of inspiration and insight. If you only take time to connect with your deeper power when in crisis or faced with a major decision, you may well find that the line has been disconnected or that there is so much mind-chatter that you cannot decipher the message. When you make listening a regular part of your day, the line stays open and the connection is often clear.

Breathe

When you make time to listen, remember to breathe. Zen practice encourages mindfulness. This can be done simply by paying attention to your breathing. Tension or deep emotions tempt us to hold our breath, perhaps out of fear or a need to control. Breath takes you to center, to Essence. When you hold it, you cannot get there.

William Hanrahan, a voice teacher and communication consultant, has taught people for more than twenty years how to reconnect to their true voice through conscious breathing. He shares his experience working with a woman challenged by the process of conscious breathing:

> I said to her, "You know you are breathing as if there isn't enough. You are trying to hang on to the breath that you've got." She said, "Oh, my God! That's how I treat the rest of my life! There's never enough time, there's never enough money, there's never enough men—there's just never enough!" So breath, for her, became a metaphor for opening up other areas of her life.

Breath is more than a metaphor for life, it *is* life. When we let go of our breath, and drink it in as the infinite resource it is, we let life in. Breathe as you live. Live as you breathe. With each breath comes an opportunity to do things differently, to make new choices.

Of breathing, writer Anne Lamott shares:

> This is not something I remember to do very often, and I do not normally like to hang around people who talk about slow conscious breathing; I start to worry that a nice long discussion of aroma therapy is right around the corner. But these slow conscious breathers are on to something, because if you try to follow your breath for a while, it will ground you in relative silence.[13]

Be Simple

"Relative silence" leads us to be simple. A friend confided her struggle to connect with her Essence. "I'm trying to listen, but the crazy voices are so much louder than my inner voice!" How many times have you struggled to separate your "crazy voices" from the voice of your Essence? Busyness, fear, and urgency are only a few distractions that can cloud perception and distort your understanding of the Essential message.

Artist and educator Hans Hoffman said, "The ability to simplify means to eliminate the unnecessary so that the necessary can speak."[14] To be simple is to return to center and ask what is necessary there. Get simple; you may be surprised to find you already own what you seek.

Listen to Art, Watch Music, Taste Dance

Perhaps your life doesn't offer up much solitude. Quiet time for you is the commuter train, as you are squeezed between the window and your seatmate's laptop. There is still hope. You can practice availability anywhere, in response to any stimulus. This kind of listening will surely lead you back to your Essence, to your integrity.

For you it may be a Sunday afternoon on the couch listening to jazz, or your son's dance concert, or the neighborhood art fair. Practice receiving and allow the music to wash over you in all of its colors, the charcoal sketches to sing their song, the dance to send you its flavors. You may be surprised to discover where simple availability takes you. Openness without agenda. Being for being's sake. As you bathe yourself in this place, you will find it easier and easier to simply be in your Essence, in all of its dynamic sights, sounds, and sensations.

Listen to Your Life

Simple availability allows you to listen to your life, counseled my friend Allison over coffee one afternoon, as I grew flush with excitement telling her of a new professional development adventure I was considering. It (the adventure) was beginning to make so much noise that it would soon take more energy *not* to listen, than to accept the message.

Listen to your life's thunder, bear witness to the swelling waves, and gentlest of summer rains. When you pause a moment and step out of the way, your life offers up more than even your fantasies allowed. In time, you may find yourself no longer listening to, seeing, hearing, or feeling your Essence. One day you may discover your ultimate integrity: you have become your Essence.

---

1. Salk, 23–24.
2. Handy, p. 135.
3. Schulz, 19.
4. Ibid., 2.
5. Gribbin, 65–66, 98.
6. Frost and Yarrow, 4.
7. Ibid.
8. Adler, 15.
9. Frost and Yarrow, 1.
10. Stratford, 93.
11. Rich, 191.
12. Milton, 168.
13. Lamott, 117.
14. *Courage to Change*, 40.

**Working in New Business Opportunities** initially proved engaging for Laurie LaMantia, a ten-year employee at AT&T. She loved the intrapreneurism that came with the job (matching talented people with innovative business opportunities). In the early nineties she and her colleagues, Angela Just and Lari Washburn, were shopping their latest proposal around the company: a bed-and-breakfast hot line using the latest communications technology. Like their entrepreneurial counterparts, the group found themselves regularly pitching the idea to potential "buyers." Just as regularly, they received the same response, "Sounds like a great idea; it's just not right for us."

Rather than allow the responses to excuse them from their passion for innovation, the three began a collective "listening" process. "We spent a lot of time sitting around in Angela's backyard gazebo," related Laurie. "This was crucial incubation time. We thought of everything from soup to nuts." Out of the mix emerged a collective "What if . . ."

"What if we created a creativity center within AT&T to foster new ideas and provide an innovation resource for the entire company?" They wrote up a proposal and made a strong business case to the VP of Marketing, Gerry Butters. The three were surprised when the first response was, "Sounds great! Do it." Within months, IdeaVerse was open for business as an autonomous entity with the mission to "nurture a climate for creativity and innovation." The unique business model they designed allowed IdeaVerse to make independent decisions, move quickly, and take advantage of a wide range of international creativity resources, including touring authors, artists, and experts, and to host workshops and events that elicited responses like, "You get to do _that_ at _work_!?!" (I can attest to this; after presenting an improv workshop at IdeaVerse, I was invited to join in a workday Scary-okee Festival in celebration of Halloween.) All of IdeaVerse's activities and programs contributed to the spirit of innovation at Lucent Technologies (spun off from AT&T in 1996). LaMantia admits, "The fact that we existed was as important as the programs we delivered."

Follow Your Passion

Turn Inspiration into Action

| **THE PRINCIPLE** | Aligning espoused corporate values with day-to-day practice is one of today's biggest challenges in business. By first listening to and then following their passion, the IdeaVerse founders discovered how to align their personal values with their livelihood. In doing so, they provided Lucent with a resource to align its innovation values with action.

After several years of providing lively training programs and hosting thought- and inspiration-provoking events, IdeaVerse was cut from the corporate budget at the end of 1999. Lucent could not justify the continuation of a business unit whose product was not quantifiable, as process rarely is. Despite the disappearance of the physical space, cofounder Angela Just has high hopes that "the spirit of IdeaVerse will live on" in the many employees who benefited from its existence.

Follow Your Passion springs from *Listen to Your Essence*. How can you follow passion without knowing your Essence? Essence leads to passion. The word *enthusiasm* is a synonym for passion and comes from the Greek *enthousiasmos* or *en-theos*, "filled will God" or spirit. It is no coincidence the Hebrew word for *work* is the same as the word for *worship*: *avohah*. When you are filled with your Essence and follow its call, you cannot help but pay tribute to something bigger than yourself (whether "bigger" is community, family, or another power greater than your will) through your work.

Practicing *Listen to Your Essence* opens the door for spirit to fill us, to enthuse us. Then we need to become willing to act on these intuitions, the sometimes "still, small voices" whispering in quiet moments or when we least expect them. Theater director Mary Zimmerman says, "The only difference between a creative person and an uncreative person is that a creative person takes his or her ideas seriously." To take our ideas seriously we need to trust their source and become willing to act on them.

I Don't Know What I'm Passionate About

"How can you follow something if you don't even know what it is?" I am no longer surprised when, during a break from one of my workshops, a well-dressed mid- to upper-level manager pulls me aside with a burdened look. I once mistook this demeanor as adversarial—that they wanted to dispute one of my assertions or complain about some aspect of the program. Now I recognize it as the look of one who needs to confess. "I don't know what I'm passionate about," they reveal.

The first time this happened, I felt a worldview crumbling around me. I realized I had assumed that, at a certain point in career and financial success, people must be in touch with some fire. After all, isn't that what fueled them to their accomplishments in the first place? Looking back, I see my naïveté. If it were true that all outwardly successful people felt completely in tune with their purpose in life, the need for my work would be greatly diminished.

Because over the years I have discovered questions about passion and purpose to be widespread, I will save you and perhaps untold others the angst of a private confessional. This chapter is my response to those whose passions have not yet emerged and a celebration of those who fill their sails with passion each day. Though you will read stories of people whose lives and work changed in response to new alignments with purpose, know that you may just as likely discover *Follow Your Passion* to lead you to change the *way* you work, not *what* you do for work.

Some of us grow numb altogether to our hopes, dreams, and passions. By letting go of them, we evade the risk of disappointment. Soon we forget that we ever had the dreams. By not allowing ourselves to know what we want in the first place, we won't feel the loss or shame from not getting it.

More than a New Age, Joseph Campbell–inspired, feel-good concept, the principle *Follow Your Passion* separates those who truly want to transform the way they work from those who just want a little relief within an otherwise toxic workplace. This may require a moment of open-mindedness for those of you seriously pondering such impossible questions as, "What would happen to the world if *everyone* followed their passion?" and for those taught, "Work isn't supposed to be fun. That's why they call it work."

Do not bother yourself with questions about "everyone." Thankfully, you can only live one life at a time. Bother yourself with the question, "What if *I* followed my passion?"

The price of not doing so may be higher than you want to pay. Robin Sheerer, author of *No More Blue Mondays*, says one study concludes that more people die of heart attacks on Monday morning than on any other day of the week. (Even more sobering is that the first symptom for 50 percent of people at risk of heart-attack is sudden death.) "Stress is one of the major factors of job dissatisfaction. People feel stress when they are in positions where they aren't leading with their strengths or where they cannot find meaning in their work." Sheerer cites the phenomena of "stars" being promoted to management positions. "It seems like a logical progression, and often the star is flattered and interested in the rewards that come with management responsibility. Unfortunately, these promotions move people away from their original passion and many discover they don't even like managing people." This sets off a negative chain of events, starting with all of the people who report to the ill-suited manager and ultimately impacting the health of the company. Sheerer found a major reason why people leave her clients' companies is poor relationships with immediate supervisors. A recent Gallup poll verifies that one in four workers would fire their boss if they could. If your company is losing its top performers due to passionless management and worker participation, it's everyone's problem.

Many of us devote 70 percent of our week to our professional lives. We bring the stress and triumphs home with us. That means it can affect your loved ones, friends, communities, and, as Sheerer says, "cast a dark cloud over what should be your leisure time." Think about it. Would you accept a 70 percent dissatisfaction rate in any other area of your life? Your marriage? Your hobbies? Your education? Your living space? Well, when you put it *that* way . . .

Corporations spend millions of training dollars each year teaching idea-generation and problem-solving techniques and are surprised when results are minimal. It's really no surprise. Think about a task you least like to do, be it filing, returning calls, attending yet another meeting, or any number of things. How often are you inspired to be creative in the midst of activities that have no meaning for you?

Essential Passion

It is possible to find enjoyment in even the most mundane tasks. Following your passion means to have purpose whether you are stuffing envelopes or cleaning the toilet. When in tune with passion, you are energized by participation. Practicing someone else's passion, however, often leaves you drained.

There is an important distinction between quick fixes and Essential passions. The passion in *Follow Your Passion* is not a transitory whim or an attraction that may harm or distract you from your journey (unhealthy relationships, excessive TV, overwork, and acquiring newer and shinier possessions, to name only a few). These attractions, or more appropriately labeled *compulsions*, are not rooted in Essence; they are not filled with the life force.

The common usage of the word *passion* leads us to think of its temporal, emotional, and sensual implications. True passion may advertise itself as these things, but not necessarily. True passion is the nexus of a deep connection to purpose and a willingness to act in its fulfillment—to be a channel for it, even a servant to it. Christ's final week, and greatest personal and spiritual challenge, is referred to as "The Passion." (Note: *The* Passion, not *A* Passion.) The passion is a divine synthesis of purpose and action. Unfortunately, we are sometimes deceived by our initial rush of excitement and adrenaline into believing that false passions are the real thing.

Business is just beginning to support authentic passion in the workplace. W. Edwards Deming said, "Our prevailing system of management has destroyed our people."[1] He meant hierarchical management models focused on meeting others' expectations and avoiding mistakes at all costs. Peter Senge's model of the "learning organization" is an effective antidote to the fear and apathy engendered by the old system. Senge's model helps workers rediscover passion and the innate desire to learn and grow. One of the most important ways we learn is by making mistakes and following our passion. When it is drained from us or replaced with someone else's, we find it all but impossible to find personal meaning and fulfillment in our work.

Without passion, we easily step outside our integrity, abandoning our moral center. We may "accidentally" take home a few office supplies, make excessive personal calls from work, perhaps fudge an expense report, or engage in potentially damaging gossip. We don't need the church, a personnel policy, or boss to tell us when we have compromised our integrity; if we check in with ourselves and listen, more often than not our own moral barometer will tell us.

Without passion we simply do not care. With passion we feel ownership and a willingness to assume risk. In fact, we may not even feel we are taking risks, because we are being guided by something much more powerful than ourselves. Isn't this how being in love feels? Perhaps this is why Matthew Fox counsels us to "fall in love at least three times a day."[2] When we are in love, we are unstoppable.

There are many ways to fall in love. Passion is as necessary for a successful business negotiation as it is for creating or performing a symphony. Conductor and composer Lukas Foss deems love the essential motivation to create. "If one uses music that one does not really love, then one will not succeed in making it one's own."[3] Without passion, there is no ownership, no connection to Essence, and thus, no creativity. Robert Bone, professor of law at Boston University, encourages students in a similar manner:

> Steep yourself in the literature and the law you really want to do. If you become intimately familiar with it, enough to understand the deep level of what's going on, . . . then new ideas will just come to you.[4]

Individual and collaborative creativity is fueled by passion—an excitement for discovery and an insatiable capacity to be surprised. Most of us have had the experience Professor Bone describes. As we practice *Follow Your Passion*, ideas and inspiration flood in. Suddenly the world rallies in support, and we run into the perfect contact at our spouse's office picnic (the event we craftily tried to miss.) Perhaps a friend sends an article our way with a note saying, "Thought you might be interested in this!" and it turns out to release an insight that was the missing piece for our proposal. Or we flip channels on a rainy Sunday afternoon and discover a documentary on our favorite subject.

Follow the Crumbs

Following your passion can also be like following a trail of bread crumbs. We may not know where it will lead us or whether it's a trail at all. Sometimes the first crumb appears to us as an "Aha!" like in the following story. At other times, we simply feel a heightened engagement with life at each step along the bread-crumb trail, and where it leads seems irrelevant.

Lu enjoyed a thriving career as a professional actress in regional theater for more than fifteen years. Ever since she was a little girl she dreamed of becoming an actress, and she made every life choice based on that goal.

In the midst of her success, Lu began to get a nagging feeling that she would not be doing what she was doing much longer. She remembers feeling angry, even duped, "That wasn't part of the bargain! After all, I'd had a plan!"

She lived and worked with this discomfort for a year and grew to accept that she needed to let go of what had been the focus of her life energy, though she had no idea what was next. Lu describes it as the "first time I had nothing to pin my identity on—no external means of identifying myself." At the end of that year, and still in the midst of "not knowing what's next," the thought came to Lu: "Maybe I should see a therapist." Just as she was considering this possibility, a second thought came to her: "You should *be* a therapist." She had discovered her "what's next."

Certainly there were obstacles along the way, but Lu shared, "I now know that the perceived problems are part of the path—and they do take care of themselves. When I am off-center, I think they are there to thwart me, when, in fact, they are part of the path and moving through them propels me forward."

Like Lu, many people I interviewed spoke about passion in their lives in spiritual terms. They experience a responsibility to live a creative life, not only for their own welfare, but for the health of their families, community, and planet.

For some of us, listening and following will lead to radical external change (as it did for Lu); for others, the change may still be radical but internal—again, transforming the *way* we work, not the work we do. More important than what it looks like is how it feels. There is no prescription for practicing this principle, only a requisite willingness to let go to your life and allow it to take your breath away with surprise.

In his book, *The Universe Is a Green Dragon*, physicist Brian Swimme explores the power of passion in Nature. He noticed parallels between the sun's attraction to the earth, an electron's attraction to the nucleus, and human attractions, be they to gardening, Shakespeare, another person, exercise, or a myriad of other creative possibilities.

> *We awake to our own unique sets of attractions. So do oxygen atoms. So do protons. The proton is attracted only to certain particles. On an infinitely more complex level, the same holds true for humans: Each person discovers a field of allurements, the totality of which bears the unique stamp of that person's personality. Destiny unfolds in the pursuit of individual fascinations and interests . . . . By pursuing your allurements, you help bind the universe together.* The unity of the world rests on the pursuit of passion. *[emphasis mine]*[5]

Of course, none of us is in touch with our passion at every moment of our lives, and passion may express itself in rather mundane ways. I have gone through periods in which I felt no clear sense of passion for any endeavor. These are not depressions, but simply times when I do my work, enjoy my friends and family, and simultaneously ask, "What's next? Where will I channel my creativity now?" I call these my sensory deprivation periods, times when I listen to my Essence and get back only silence.

These periods are part of the ebb and flow of living a creative life. They are crucial, just as slow cooking is crucial to some wonderful meals. As with the slow-cooked meal, something is happening—just not something seen or experienced. I have learned not to force this time, but to trust that the silence is telling me to "keep on keeping on." Passion eventually does rise to the top of my creative Crock-Pot, and I am ready to embrace it then (something I could not have done had it revealed itself any earlier).

Some of us, however, are hindered in following our passion because of our learned blocks.

| LEARNED BLOCKS |

Keep Enthusiasm in Check

We cut ourselves off from passion in much the same way we cut ourselves off from Essence, with busyness, distraction, and second-guessing. At these times we faithfully do our best to keep our enthusiasm in check. To get excited is to risk ridicule. Passion is messy, loud, and nonlinear—a threat to others desperately trying to keep their own in check.

Sometimes we are more comfortable with people in crisis or great pain than with people experiencing joy and passion. We tell our enthusiastic friends we are happy for them, yet secretly feel relieved when they return their attention to life's mundane challenges and disappointments.

If we do not follow our own passion, the passion of others can actually cause us pain. And if we spend much time around others who are not following their passion, keeping ours in check is reinforced. We may even ridicule those cracking open the door to let their spirit rush in and enthuse them. Perhaps you have been witness to or victim of the following dysfunctional workplace phenomenon: An energetic new hire joins your team or department. She comes from another company or industry and is brimming with suggestions and ideas for improvement, much to the irritation of the seasoned employees. Within weeks or months she is beaten down by the choruses of "We don't do it that way here." To survive she must either accept the passionless culture or leave; either alternative is an enormous loss.

Shame

It is said that if we are not part of the solution, we are part of the problem. When we do not practice Follow Your Passion, we become part of the problem. Here we discovered *shame*.

Shame is a learned response based on a distorted belief system, a mythology of "shoulds." When we think we should make more money; we should be over that loss; we should have gotten another degree; we should have more, do more, be more; we are swept up in the funnel cloud of shame. It lifts us off our center, spins us around, and flings us far off course. Rooted in the internalization of others' expectations or imagined social authority, shame dictates to us what is "right," and, more important, what is "wrong."

Shame blocks us from the knowledge of our passion and needs in ways large and small. I was at a spiritual retreat in a beautiful wooded area some years ago. A small lake, hiking trails, horses, and various other outdoor adventures beckoned. I love the outdoors and am often the first one to jump in whenever there is a body of water nearby. This retreat, however, was different. I only wanted to sleep. Despite my mysterious exhaustion, I dragged myself to the meetings and meals, and made a valiant attempt at socializing. At one session I shared my frustration with my fatigue and struggle to participate. After a silence, the workshop leader gently responded, "What would happen if you slept as much as you needed?"

What an idea! I was so caught up in participating the right way, that it had not occurred to me to listen to my body and rest as much as I needed. (I now see the irony here; at a spiritual retreat, I was ignoring the voice of my spirit!) Ever since, I have found many opportunities to ask versions of the workshop leader's question. What would happen if I submitted that proposal, registered for that sign language class, took those sailing lessons, went to that conference? In other words, what would happen if I *listened* to my Essence and *followed* my passion? Could I be stalled by another learned block?—be practical?

Practicality

Inspiration often comes in odd packages. This can be a bit scary. Most of us would like to know the outcome of our actions in advance—that's only practical, right? Not only is it not practical, it's not possible and won't transform the way you work. Wanting to know the end at the beginning is a sign that you are limited by the causal, mechanistic worldview—one that will assure you that if you input A, B and C, you will get X, Y and Z.

I tried to work that way. As an undergraduate theater student, I focused intense energy on building experience and skills as a stage manager (one who oversees the needs of production, rehearsals, and performance). I thought that was practical. I would have marketable skills and a list of professional credits to my name and would be able to make a relatively good living upon graduation. There was one hitch, summed up best by a T-shirt I recently saw, which read: "What I really want to do is direct."

I, chose, however, to direct on the sly, pursuing my passion by directing late-night shows with intern companies at regional theaters and watching other directors work. To be sure, this was a wonderful education for a young director. However, as the years passed, I found myself stifled by others' perceptions of me as a manager and not an artist.

Most debilitating to my creative spirit was my self-perception. How we view ourselves has a powerful effect on how much of our creativity we express. Once I shifted my energy back to my original passion, I became restored to my creativity. Ironically, my years as a director ended up being the most practical of all, for without them I never would have discovered my current work. Today I have a deeper integration of passion in my life and work than ever before.

Ben Hollis, a TV producer and musician, went through a similar transformation in the way he works. He calls his version of "be practical" the "professionalisation" of his creative process. "As soon as I got a new idea," he told me, "the wheels would start to turn and I would begin to think, 'How can I market this? How will I be able to make money off of this?'" Those impulses lurk beneath the surface for many of us; we try to make sense of the process or decide on the viability of our ideas well before we give them chances to take shape.

Risk

There are many ways to follow your passion and still keep a roof over our heads. Lu continued to work as an understudy, drawing a paycheck while freeing up time to complete her second master's degree. The universe loves to support those who live to their full potential and pursue dreams. It asks only that we trust we will be taken care of, even when we cannot imagine how. This is a challenge if we have also learned "Don't take risks."

As "be practical"'s partner in crime, this block tells us that anything that takes us into the unknown is dangerous and perhaps fatal. Little support exists for risk-taking, for letting go of something we have in order to get something we want. Emotional, physical, and spiritual risks bring with them the possibilities of loss. Sometimes we risk losing something we are convinced we cannot live without.

Some years ago I was certain I needed to own a Ford Explorer. Persistence brought me and my vehicular soul mate together. For three years I enjoyed many adventures in my Explorer. Then the possibility arose that I might have to give up the car. I needed to raise cash to finish the research on a project I had been working on for some time. Selling the car looked like the best option. I would be taking a risk and knew it. Would I ever own such a nice car again? Would I ever own any car again? Would I adjust to getting around the city on my bike and public transportation? What if I sold the car and the project failed? Then I would have no car and no dream. I drove myself to distraction with all of the "what ifs." Then one day I knew I was ready to let go of the car. I could not afford to take on extra work to raise the cash, because that would leave no time for my project. I knew I couldn't afford to let go of my dream, for then I would truly be broke. What happened with the project? You are reading it, and I have become an avid cyclist.

All of us are challenged to take risks and let go of comfort (even if we know it isn't good for us), in order to grow and make room for more abundance. We let go of relationships, jobs, living arrangements, eating habits, hairstyles, cars, and all kinds of attachments. We take a leap of faith. We have to take the risk of letting go, before the universe will reveal what it has in mind to replace what we let go of, before the quantum leap will occur. This isn't easy for us—we want to see what's behind door number three before we give up our year's supply of Eskimo Pies. That's risky.

We may fear actually getting what we want more than we fear not achieving our dreams—for then we might have to be happy! Can we risk that much goodness, that much *enthus*iasm in our lives? Will we recognize ourselves in this joy? Will others? Perhaps that is just what we need to do—re-*cognize* ourselves as channels of our deepest passion.

If we practice *Listen to Your Essence*, then we can trust our passion to be true. As we allow ourselves to feel the rush of excitement, anticipation, and curiosity, we are swept away by discovery. There is nothing to lose if we approach our passion as humble students; all we risk is the possibility of learning from our experiences. When we practice Follow Your Passion, it appears that we choose a life of risk, but if we value our vision above an illusion of security, we have nothing to lose by pursuing it. Vision cannot be lost or taken away, unless we choose to lose it or give it away. Our reward may be new experiences, joy, passion, and finding ourselves in uncharted territories where our world defines itself according to new rules, or according to no rules at all. This will challenge those of us practicing perfectionism.

Perfectionism

My friend Peter decided to heed his inner rumblings and signed up for that yoga class he had been thinking about for months. He sent in the registration fee, bought new sweatpants, and headed to the community center for his first class. The room was cozy, and the instructor had lowered the lights and lit incense. Peter took a deep breath and gave himself over to the experience.

The instructor encouraged the students not to worry about doing it right. "This is not a competition," she said, "Keep your attention on your own experience and your own journey." The first exercise she demonstrated was the "Salute to the Sun." Peter followed her lead and soon became frustrated. His legs were stiff from years of sitting in front of a computer terminal. He couldn't even touch the floor with his fingertips (and he couldn't help but notice the instructor's hands were flat on the ground, as were a few of the other supposed beginners). By the end of the class Peter felt more tense than when he came in. He felt he had failed.

Soon after the first class he recognized that his perfectionism had cut himself off from the experience. He later told me of his life-long obsession, "If I can't do it perfectly, then I don't want to try at all. If I can't be Mother Teresa, then I don't even want to be nice to people." I encouraged him to go back, citing advice given to me when I was learning sign language: "Anything worth doing, is worth doing badly."

When we give ourselves permission to be awkward beginners, we have the opportunity to make new discoveries. "Experts" may struggle to take in new information. The beginner is an empty cup ready to be filled. If we expect perfection from ourselves in every endeavor, we will never find the creative opportunity; we will be too focused on getting it right to recognize inspiration, even if it hits us over the head.

Other People

Despite the possibilities for where passion can lead us in business, we may have learned to give our creative power to other people. Other people can be formidable obstacles in our pursuit of passion. Naysayers, energy-drainers, and enviers all provide excellent distractions. They prevent us from following or even knowing our passion. We are in dangerous territory when we give other people that much power. A wise woman said, "If the other person is the problem, there is no solution." As long as we blame other people for our circumstances, we have no power to change them. When the problem is out *there*, we avoid responsibility for it. We choose not to respond.

Tired of the outdated and cumbersome process of tracking and processing orders, Dina decided to design a new database for her regional office. "I was sick of complaining to my supervisor. I finally shut up and got to work." The database and streamlined process became a model for the entire corporation. Dina was surprised to return from vacation to discover that she had won an award for her work.

When we ask what we ourselves can change about our experience, we have power again. We are no longer victims. This is an incredibly liberating experience. And freedom comes, in part, by doing things differently.

| DOING THINGS DIFFERENTLY |

Ask for Help

Sometimes the simplest possibilities elude us: we forget to ask for help. Seek the company of people who celebrate your passion. One of the most valuable lessons in my own journey is that I cannot do it alone, and since I've begun doing things differently I have wondered why would I want to? After all, no one ever accomplished anything great without help.

Help comes in many forms and from unexpected places. I have found just the solutions I needed from enthusiastic reference librarians, my clients, students, fellow writers, teaching colleagues, gas station attendants, professional speaking colleagues, and many others. We never know where our mentors are until we seek them. They are hard-pressed to help us if we don't ask!

For those battling the voices of fear and judgment on a daily basis, help is available in formal and informal relationships. Many workplaces today have mentorship programs designed to support professional development. Or you may choose to find your own "creative buddy," a "partner in possibility"—someone to listen to your musings and to take along for the test drive of your new ideas. Whether formal or informal, these relationships can provide just the antidote to doubt and fear.

"Bookending" (following up on commitments to yourself) with a friend, mentor, or buddy provides accountability, which in turn fosters responsibility to our creative process. In the early stages of our creative recovery we may not take seriously the commitments we whisper to ourselves, but we might honor those we say out loud to a trusted supporter who will want to know whether or not we followed through.

One of the first creativity workshops I led has continued to meet on its own for years. Its members share works-in-progress and lives-in-progress, and enthusiastically support each others' professional successes, gallery openings, and performances (a few years ago many of these people would not have dared to call themselves creative!). The group is a collective creative buddy that inspires passion. Some workplaces are sponsoring such informal groups with similar results.

Weed Out Saboteurs

At the same time you seek support for passion, weed out those well-meaning saboteurs who rain on your parade. There is a difference between the honest, loving responses of trusted friends (which gives us an opportunity to determine whether or not we have been swept away by a quick-fix passion) and the veiled remarks of those ultimately threatened by your passion.

Follow Fear

The most supportive response is often to follow your fear. Follow my fear? Yes, fear often indicates that you are close to creative paydirt. Fear of a challenge may require you to reach to new professional heights, fear of a discovery may change your direction, or fear of a breakthrough may lead to a new level of self-knowledge.

Years ago I was invited to speak at a national conference on creativity. Until then, I had comfortably presented seminars to businesspeople, educators, and nonprofit groups. These people were always thirsty for what I had to say, and rarely were there any creativity authorities present. Suddenly I was going to be reviewed by others who were experts in the field! I rose to the occasion by focusing on my message and the aspects unique to my work. It turned out to be a wonderful, reaffirming experience that allowed me to take my own work to a new level. I (and they) would have missed an important opportunity had I given in to my self-centered fear.

Most of us have had similar experiences. Of course we will be afraid of the unknown, the new experiences, the big challenges. But if you allow it, fear will be your divining rod, homing in on the mother lode of your creative process.

Think of fear as a big ugly creature, frothing at the mouth, wildly waving its tentacles as it guards the door of your passion. It wants you to believe that what lurks behind that door is even worse than itself. It does take courage to walk through that door, because what awaits is the opportunity to step into your life and experience yourself in a way you never dreamed possible. You might even discover what it is like to be happy. *Then* what would you have to complain about?

Fear is a subversive smoke screen that impedes forward movement. Underneath may lie your deepest passion. Remember, courage is fear meeting faith. Feel the fear and Follow *Your* Passion. Value your ideas and inspirations. Don't wait around for someone else to encourage you or drag you to that graduate school orientation, management seminar, or Israeli folk dance you want to attend.

Give your passion the space and support it needs. Essence is the source of inspiration. Passion is the source of action. When your Essence inspires your curiosity and gives you joy, heed the call. Jeff Tworek found the courage to follow his passion, despite the warnings of friends and family:

> *A few years ago I heard about and saw a company and product that made my heart start to race. I had been employed by a Fortune-50 company for thirteen years, where I had a very successful career. Upon seeing this new revolutionary technology, I was drawn to it like a moth to a flame. I could not stop thinking about it and how right my background was for selling it. I told my family about it and they thought that I was crazy for even thinking about leaving my current employer. My burning desire to be involved with this new company continued, and I made up my mind to get hooked-up with them. I knew it was going to be difficult to get a job with this company because of its high profile and popularity, but for some reason everything magically fell into place. It has been two years since I made this move to this company, and it has been wildly successful and more rewarding than I ever could have imagined. I owe this all to following my passion and not listening to the voices of fear and judgment.*

Though tempted, Jeff was connected enough to his own Essence to not allow others' fears distort his vision. He also did not mistake someone else's passion for his own.

Look for the Lightning

"That's great for you, Jeff, Lu, and all those others," you say, "but I don't have any driving force in my life today. How can I follow something I just don't feel?" Perhaps you haven't looked in the right places. Perhaps you need to look for the lightning. As you reflect on the storms and clear days of your life, you will surely remember some electricity. When do you remember yourself at your happiest and most engaged? Is there a time in your life, or a fleeting moment, when you were most content, at peace with yourself and the universe, exactly where you were supposed to be, doing just what you were meant to do? It might have been a childhood summer at the lake, a work or community project that energized you, a teaching or coaching opportunity, or any number of large or small endeavors. Make a list of these events. Choose two or three and write them out in detail; tell the stories.

Let them sit for a few days, then read your stories as if you were reading about someone else's life. You may even want to ask a trusted friend (here's a good job for your mentor or creativity buddy) to read it, too, as if it was about someone they didn't know. What did the stories have in common? Perhaps they all took place outdoors, or involved children, or were highly collaborative, or gave you complete autonomy. What values does this person have? Is this a person who values education and community? Financial security and material abundance? Health and adventure? Aah . . . a picture is starting to emerge. Let it reflect your passion back to you. Let the common threads weave your tapestry.

Wherever you are in your quest to live a passionate life, check in from time to time and ask yourself what your life would look like if you had nothing to prove. Would it look the same? What changes would you make? What resources do you need to make those changes?

Find the Higher Value

Many people would not choose to change their work itself, but would rather change their relationship to their work. For those of you put off by the implication that following your passion may take you away from the life you love, take heart in Cyril's example and find the higher value in your work.

For years I have been impressed with the excellent service and good humor of my postal carrier. Cyril embodies the "neither blinding snow or driving rain . . ." philosophy, but he doesn't just get the mail there, he smiles, always has a friendly word, and repeatedly goes out of his way to be sure that my high-maintenance mail and I find our way to each other. I have not been singled out for this special treatment. Tales of Cyril's feats are legendary in the neighborhood.

One day I asked him what motivated him to go so far beyond the call of duty on a daily basis, when he could just as easily keep his job if he put in half the effort. He was surprised that I was making such a big deal out of his service, even though he has received numerous awards for it. At first he said, "I don't know. It's my job, I just try to do the best I can." I didn't let him off so easily; it was 4:30 P.M. and I had caught him making a second attempt that day to deliver a neighbor's package, though many of his colleagues would have slapped a sticky note on the door after the first try and been on their way home. "I guess I just think of how I would feel if it was my mail. I'd want someone to go the extra mile for me." Passion puts your higher values of service, excellence, friendliness, community, and innovation into action.

Maybe you will discover your true passion has little to do with your livelihood. Your passion for mountain biking, listening to klezmer bands, or collecting salt and pepper shakers connects you to your life in a way that perhaps only you can understand. It creates room for your spirit to play and for quantum leaps, and may well breathe life into your work. Trying to professionalize it would dry up this well, as Ben Hollis taught us.

The road of passion may not always be pothole-free. The more powerful the path, in terms of potential for personal growth and success, the more vigorously the universe may challenge your commitment to it and offer you excuses to throw in the towel. But, as my fortune read after a recent Chinese meal, "Your path is difficult, but you will be amply rewarded."

Sometimes the reward will be the path itself and the exhilaration of full participation in your life. When Leonardo daVinci was asked to name his greatest achievement, he responded, "Leonardo daVinci." Follow your passion and receive the amplest reward of all—yourself.

---

1. Senge, Video.
2. Fox, 19.
3. Keeva, 52–53.
4. Ibid.
5. Swimme, 47–48.

There was a problem: the manufacturing company Frank worked for had purchased four million dollars worth of equipment—before the job for which it was ordered was approved. Now four million dollars sat in the warehouse taking up space and not producing a profit. After thirty years Frank had worked his way up to a comfortable (his shop floor buddies would say "cushy") management position. Though solving this problem was not his direct responsibility, comfort didn't keep Frank from being bothered by the waste of idle machinery, so he and a few of his staff met to discuss possible uses for the equipment. They reviewed a number of projects on the production docket and found a few that could be run on two of the new machines, thus freeing up other machines and increasing overall production time. After running the numbers and completing the assessment, Frank wrote his suggestion in an E-mail memo to his supervisor (who *was* responsible for this problem).

He looked forward to the executive response to his team's initiative. When it came, he wished he hadn't bothered. The reply memo read, "We've already considered other uses for the equipment. But what I really want to know is how much time you and your staff wasted coming up with these ideas."

ABSTAIN FROM JUDGMENT

Remove Blocks to Creativity

| **THE PRINCIPLE** | I wish I could report that Frank's story was a blemish on an otherwise porcelain business innovation report. Unfortunately, when I share this story with business audiences, I see more nods of recognition than gasps of shock. The stark truth is that, despite all the talk about creativity, innovation, and new approaches to familiar challenges, most people have no idea how to foster it in themselves, let alone their organizations. Even more infuriating, these same unwitting enemies of creativity wonder why their staff don't return from the latest creativity seminar brimming with new ideas—final proof, they surmise, that their people simply are not creative.

Seeds of Creative Disability

My life's work is to set the record straight and help people get out of the way of the creative potential all around. Countercreative, judgment is the most insidious block to innovation. Most of us have had at least one experience that shut down all or part of our passion. Self-judgment, censorship, criticism, and merciless comparison damage as much as does the judgment of others. For many, the seeds of creative disability were planted early.

As a young girl, Susan saved her allowance to buy the paint set she had spotted in the neighborhood dime store. After her secret mission, Susan slipped down to the basement with her shiny new supplies. A Peg-Board wall served as a makeshift easel. Soon Susan was immersed in the world of painting. She spent hours in her private artist's cove. She hurried home from school and got up early on weekends to make time for her passion, away from the relentless teasing of four sisters.

One day at her school library Susan saw an art book filled with the work of van Gogh, O'Keeffe, Duchamp, Kahlo, and other masters. She eagerly brought the book home and poured over it. As she stared at the work of those who had spent their lives developing art, her heart sank. Eight-year-old Susan looked at those beautiful, detailed paintings in the book, and then at her own watercolors. In a moment, she decided the work that had been the source of such joy and passion was in fact a horrible waste of time—and a dismal failure. She closed the library art book and crumpled up her paintings, burying them deep in the laundry room trash can. She put away her paint set for the last time and slipped back upstairs—unnoticed.

Judgment destroys the wonder so necessary to create space for possibilities. Without wonder we would still live in the dark ages. Discovery propels us forward. We are all born with a desire to play; that's how we learned about ourselves and our world. That is how we continue to learn. We forget that.

Tammy, a project manager for a construction firm, discovered the profound impact of judgment on her life. "I spent the better part of my life judging myself and, therefore, my creativity as lacking. . . . What allowed me to recognize the creativity I'd possessed all along was finally becoming sick and tired of seeking approval from outside of myself."

The Creative Process

Scientists continue to search for consistency within the largely unpredictable subatomic world. Likewise, though the creative process is nonlinear and defies compartmentalization, it is helpful to consider it in terms of three equally important stages: generation, evaluation, and implementation. These stages tend to be most useful in discussing applied innovation, where the problem or challenge (e.g., improving customer service or cutting costs) is initially clear. The connections apply to our wider discussion of creativity, as well.

Generation. I liken this stage to an open faucet, where we allow our ideas to flow freely, without fear of censorship from ourselves or others. This stage may also include valuable incubation time where new ideas are nurtured into clarity. Brainstorming, one of the oldest idea-generation techniques, occurs in this stage of the creative process.

Evaluation. Here we step back and take a look at our buckets full of ideas and options. We decide which are innovative and worth exploring, cost-effective, or simply seem like fun. We also decide which ideas need more incubation. All creative processes, even improvisation, pass through the evaluation stage. Whether it happens in a split second or over months of deliberation, it is a pivotal focusing stage of the creative process. In formal idea-generation sessions, it is crucial that the evaluation criteria be articulated before beginning this stage.

Implementation. This third and often overlooked stage is where the rubber meets the road; here we do the footwork to bring passion to life. Businesses lament the failure of their creativity training, disappointed that the wonderful ideas developed there do not make it into practice. This is often due to a breakdown in the implementation stage, which is characterized by confusion and lack of accountability.

These three stages have equal value. Trouble begins when we give more value to one than to another, rushing through the generation stage in order to get on with the evaluation stage. Even more damaging is evaluating or judging our ideas while still in the generation stage, before the ideas are fully formed. Author Judith Guest says, "The 'creator' and the 'editor'—two halves of the writer whole—should sleep in separate rooms."[2] We censor our impulses as stupid or impractical before we have even begun to explore their possibilities. This abuses and destroys the creative process; we simply cannot simultaneously judge and be receptive to possibilities.

Generation-stage critical judgment is like a gardener who, in her desire to grow champion tomatoes, evaluates each plant's potential just as it peeks through the soil, and chooses at that point either to destroy or nurture each seedling.

We call parents who are critical of their children "unreasonable," at best, and "abusive," at worst. These external voices of judgment are soon internalized, played over and over again into adulthood. Tammy remembers, "Prior to confronting my father's alcoholism and our family response to it, I spent a great deal of time in self-criticism and had a very low value of myself—the essential part of me."

Dianna described the effect of her self-judgment in team meetings at work:

I would harshly judge every opinion I had before voicing it. If the idea survived my barrage of questioning, fault-finding, and measuring up to everyone else's comments, then I would voice the

idea. Needless to say, I did not participate too much at meetings.
I rarely attacked others' ideas with the same venom I used on
myself.

We clearly see the destructive power of judgment here, yet we commit the same crimes against our own creative process without batting an eye. "That's a crazy idea!" "No one will respect you again if you say that!" "You're too old to try that!" Or, "You're too young to try that!" We say to ourselves what we would never dream of saying to a loved one or to someone whom we want to support.

Michael Ray and Rochelle Myers call these negative messages the "voj" (Voice of Judgment).[3] In *Writing Down the Bones*, Natalie Goldberg calls her censor "the editor,"[4] while people recovering from the addictive process simply say, "That's the disease talking." Whatever name you choose for this destructive self-talk, know that these messages are not true. They are not you.

Abstain from Judgment is rooted in the wisdom of recovery programs. An alcoholic knows that the first step toward recovery is to stop drinking, to abstain from the behavior that is causing so much pain. Only then will there be room for life to rush in. Likewise, we must first stop judging in order for the full resources of our imagination to become available.

Quantum physicists have discovered that judgment (or more appropriately, scientific expectation) profoundly affects the outcome of subatomic particle experiments. Before being measured, particles cannot be said to have a specific momentum or location (as discussed earlier). This is not because the scientists or their equipment are inadequate; it is simply the nature of the subatomic world, which is expressed in terms of potential and probability.

In particle experiments, when information about the momentum of an electron is sought, only general information about the location can be obtained. Likewise, the more accurately the location is measured, the less accurately the momentum can be measured, according to the Heisenberg uncertainty principle. Observing the atom disturbs it. Therefore the outcome of the observation is affected. It is impossible for the observer *not* to participate in or influence the world he observes.

The observer's or participant's relationship to the subatomic world mirrors our relationship to the early stages of the creative process. Before we judge, impulses and ideas have unlimited potential. They are processes, rather than products, and each possibility is as viable as the next. As soon as we place a value judgment, we narrow the possibilities for expression.

A study published in the *Harvard Business Review* calls this phenomenon in the workplace the "Set-Up-to-Fail Syndrome." Researchers noted how management's tendency to categorize employees based on superficial or circumstantial performance criteria often became a self-fulfilling prophecy. The downward spiral was set in motion and sometimes exacerbated when the employee tried to counter negative perceptions.[5] Here the judge had a tangible limiting effect on the judged.

Paralyzing Assumptions

This chapter could have been titled "Abstain from Assumptions." Assumptions are beliefs usually not based in fact but in bias, experience, or socialization. Not surprisingly, most definitions of the word include "arrogance." When we make assumptions or presumptions, we arrogantly believe that our way is the right way because—well, because it is. We have seen the impact of assumption in science and on individual creativity. In a social world, assumptions (learned blocks) define the world of its inhabitants, limiting what can be created within it.

Evaluation and measurement do have a place in the creative process, but not in the first generation stage. The words *evaluation*, *judgment*, and *criticism* are usually associated with a spectrum of value judgments. The value judgments (as in "That's a [*fill in the blank*] idea!") make creative flow grind to a halt. As soon as we label an idea "stupid," "out-dated," "horrible," or even: "fabulous," "brilliant," "innovative," we limit its potential.

Improvisation is an art form of the generation stage. Seasoned improvisers channel their creativity and encourage fellow players to heighten and explore discoveries on stage. George Badecker, a New York performer and improvisation teacher, sees the impact of judgment on his students.

> *There's this issue of wanting to be funny. I see people checking themselves and instead of following their first impulse, which may be the more interesting, dramatic or moving possibility, I see them trying to be funny rather than going with their instinct. They have a preconceived notion that improvisation has to be funny, and they censor anything that doesn't fit that notion.*

How often have you, like novice improvisers, censored your speech or actions because you thought you knew in advance what was expected or "right" for the situation? Judgment paralyzes. Abstaining from judgment removes the obstacles to the natural and passionate flow of your creativity. To free yourself of these chains, you need to fiercely confront your learned blocks.

| LEARNED BLOCKS |

Criticizing Others

I once believed that I could increase my value—my status—by criticizing others. Perhaps I misunderstood, but I thought the saying was "If you can't say something critical, don't say anything at all." Life was a competition, and criticism was one of my most effective weapons to diminish the perceived opponents. Judgment, or assigning value to people and their ideas, provides an illusion of having power over others. The problem is just that: it is an illusion.

Furthermore, judging others sets the cycle of limited possibilities in motion. David Cooperrider, professor of organizational behavior at Case Western Reserve University and the creator of an anti-problem-solving method called "Appreciative Inquiry," says, "Once we describe something as a problem, we assume that we know what the ideal is—what should be—and we go in search of ways to close any 'gaps'—not to expand our knowledge or build better ideals."[6]

I honed my formidable problem-defining skills as an undergraduate theater student, watching countless productions and participating in as many formal (and informal) critique sessions. We students were trained in the fine art of criticism. We learned the elements that comprised a "successful" production and attended shows like vultures, waiting for friends and colleagues to slip up, so we could feast on their shortcomings at postshow discussions.

These sessions were rarely for the benefit of the creators, but for us, the student observers, to prove how much we knew and that, if the offending production had been in our hands, we certainly would have avoided the obvious mistakes our classmates had made.

Liz Lerman, the founding director of the Dance Exchange in Washington, D.C., has spent many years thinking about new ways to respond to emerging ideas. She has developed a method called the Critical Response Process (CRP), now used by creative collaborators in many fields.

The more I worked as a choreographer, the fewer people I trusted to tell me about my work, since much of what I received in the form of criticism from others seemed to tell me more about their biases and expectations than about the particular dance of mine being discussed. It didn't seem to me to really be about helping me to make the best dance I could from my own imagination. At

the same time, it seemed that the more I saw of other peoples'
work, the more it became clear to me that what I criticized in
their work was that it wasn't like mine. If I didn't see my own
ideas confirmed in the work of others, I found myself being very
critical—my critical comments told me more about myself than
about the nature of the work I was seeing.

David! Liz! Where were you when I needed you? My classmates and I did not learn about the generation stage of the creative process or about appropriate response. Nor were we taught the role of failure in the development of our work. Rather, we learned the adage You are only as good as your last show. Almost every profession has an equivalent saying, "You are only as good as your last [*case, book, sale, presentation, project, etc.*]" To our detriment, we did not learn the difference between judgment and clear response (see this chapter's Doing Things Differently).

Sadly, I was not alone in my experience. Students and professionals in almost every domain suffer from an obsession with rooting out imperfection.

Judging Yourself

Mara, a lawyer and artist, remembers her law school training and its impact on her creative life:

Law is taught by the Socratic method. This is about testing some-
one from every angle. We would stand up in class and be grilled
about a case. We were always on the watch for something that
we'd done wrong or said wrong. Law schools justify how they
train us, because it's how they believe we will experience it out-
side . . . mistakes can be very dramatic in law. I can understand
why we lawyers are so cautious, because the stakes are so high, and
the standard is perfection. The result is that we become our own
judges. This cuts us off from seeing all of the possibilities.

Mara, like so many others, learned that the sharp blade (or tongue) of judgment cuts both ways. We cannot use it on others without injuring ourselves in the process, because we also learned to "Judge your own ideas first before anyone else has a chance."

This process begins innocently; we learned it was impolite to blow our own horn. That soon turned into our inability to accept compliments from others, which then evolved into full-blown self-criticism. Many times I have found myself in a rehearsal, or other creative process, distracted by the negative reviews the committee in my head was writing, or putting words to the most vicious self-criticism.

Self-abuse is a powerful distraction. Linna, who embraced her passion for dance later in life, finds in her spirituality freedom from self-judgment and the judgment of others. "When I listen to and obey my higher power, I move forward. There is no conflict. When I mistakenly believe I need to please other people, that's when I get confused and lose my way."

At first self-criticism seems a useful shelter from the criticism of others. After all, if we shoot down our own ideas first, we won't have to suffer the pain of hearing the judgment that we imagine will come from others.

Just as Susan decided that her early paintings didn't measure up to the masters, we too, find reasons to abort our early, awkward, and unformed ideas. If we find evidence to support our fear that we are not the next Madame Curie or George Washington Carver (and who couldn't find such evidence in the formative stages of any pursuit?), we put ourselves out of our misery by letting go of our passion altogether.

Approval

We may also distract ourselves by asking "How am I doing so far?" We become entertainers furiously tap-dancing with sweat pouring, limbs flying—desperately trying to please the audience. When we look up from the generation stage to see if we have approval from whomever we've assigned that role, we abandon the process. Our creativity becomes about listening to someone else's Essence rather than our own. We must delight ourselves before we can hope to move others.

Grandiosity and Atrocity

Judgment may also rear its ugly head disguised as grandiosity or atrocity. We ride the judgment pendulum to its extremes; one extreme leads to riches and *Oprah* appearances, the other to public humiliation. When we are in this destructive cyclone, it is uncanny how much evidence we find to propel us to new heights of tortured (and, thankfully, distorted) thinking.

After my business creativity seminars I sometimes ask participants to fill out evaluation sheets so that I can continue to improve. Early in my career, the temptation was to interpret each comment as wildly positive or brutally negative. An innocent "Great workshop! You are an intelligent and inspiring speaker," fostered visions of hosting my own TV program, while a "Needed more time for the exercises and discussion," had me reconsidering my life's work altogether. Had I only known about the third option—to take in the response only if it was useful, and stay on course toward my own personal vision and passion—I might have saved myself from this self-obsessed waste of time.

Both extremes of the pendulum destroy the joy of the process. Both cut us off from a full experience of what is. Grandiosity and atrocity also place us at the imagined center of the universe. Even self-abusive thoughts ultimately are self-centered as in, "I'm the biggest piece of doo-doo the world ever revolved around." These distorted, self-centered thoughts, however, only serve to take us out of our true center and away from our Essence. They also derail us from making any useful contributions to our organizations, communities, families, or ourselves.

Assigning Value

We will also be thrown off center if we assign value to emerging ideas. As we now know, there is a place for evaluating the merits of our creative impulses—*after* we give full attention to the generation stage. Evaluating may be editing, revising, reworking, discussing, or simply letting go of ideas about which we feel less passion. None of these processes should assign value to the work itself. Doing so can severely impact the creator, as well as the creative process. We have seen how ideas and their custodians are limited and distorted in the face of judgment.

Despite businesses' dismal record of fostering new ideas, there is hope in even the most carnivorous workplace. Everyone has opportunities to abstain from judgment, whether deciding how to promote volunteer participation, generating ideas to increase company profits, or resolving a team conflict due to years of training and practice in judgment, we do not always seize these opportunities. But we can break free by doing things differently.

| DOING THINGS DIFFERENTLY |

Distinguish Between Judgment and Response

The mechanistic model thrives on dualism; either we judge emerging ideas, or we don't say anything at all and are at the mercy of ideas and impulses with all levels of merit. A third option, however, is to distinguish between judgment and response. While judgment assigns value to the idea or its source, response provides useful information to the recipient. Response acknowledges the necessity of participation for creativity and provides fuel for cocreation (and I believe all creation is cocreation).

Again, we learn from the physicists who discovered that the very act of observation influenced what they observed. Today we acknowledge there is rarely such a thing as a truly objective observer. Subatomic physicists, social scientists, and documentary filmmakers unavoidably impact their subjects. In the arts, the viewer is often thought of as a participant as well as an observer in the creation of the collective experience.

Whereas judgment-laden response focuses on the object as separate from the observer, clear response focuses on the experience of the observer as participant and does not assume that the observer-participant's perception is the only one possible.

Note the difference between: (1) "That's a ridiculous idea! You're too old to learn a whole new industry," and (2) "I'm surprised by your idea. It would be hard for me to learn a new industry at this point."

Stating opinions or fears as facts is all too easy. But when we speak in terms of our own experience, we keep the focus on ourselves without threatening the collaborative process or passing judgment. Feedback is as essential to the evolution of any creative process as it is to natural systems traveling through seemingly chaotic stages. If the response or the responder, however, is given too much power, we can be thrown off center and lose touch with our own instincts and Essence. We all see our experiences in the context of our personal worldviews. This makes for a wonderful diversity of perspectives.

Ask for Appropriate Response

It is confusing when we forget there may be more than one response to evolving ideas. We need to ask for appropriate response. Received prematurely, even the clearest, most well-intentioned response distracts, at best, or destroys, at worst. In the development stages of a new play, I would invite a few trusted observers to witness the evolving work. During the early generation stage of development, I did not want detailed responses about the outward manifestation of the piece. I wanted general responses to the spirit and general shape of the story, and the textures of the piece. I saved the details for the evaluation stage, when we would edit, shape, and polish.

Liz Lerman suggests that the creator first accept affirmations about the work or idea. No matter how unorthodox, there is always something to applaud in an emerging idea. First hearing, "I liked the colors you used in the cost-benefit analysis chart," or "Our clients love the individual attention you suggest," opens the creator up to receiving feedback in the spirit of collaboration.

Next Lerman coaches the creator(s) to ask questions of the audience. "Was the benefit to the client clear to you?" "Do you see how this supports our mission?" This is time for the creator to get specific information necessary to continue the development process. It is not intended to evaluate viability.

Refuse to Judge Emerging Ideas

It took me several uncomfortable experiences to learn to ask for the appropriate response for the generation stage, as well as to refuse to judge emerging ideas. Again, this does not mean that we don't step back at the appropriate time to evaluate our ideas and decide which ones deserve our energy. We do continue, however, to abstain from assigning value judgments of good or bad.

Rather than find the flaws in the infant idea, you can turn negative reactions into constructive feedback. For example, instead of saying, "I don't see how we can take this project any further; it clearly is too expensive," search for the positive spin, "I'd like to see how we can make this plan more cost-effective so it will fit into next year's budget." Focusing on solutions is a wonderful way to give a clear response without judging either the idea or its owner.

Abstain from Judgment

Another strategy with roots in Lerman's Critical Response Process is to encourage the audience to ask questions of the creator. Initially the questions may be inspired by judgments, but are re-presented for the benefit of the creator. For example, an initial audience response of "We tried something like that two years ago and it failed miserably," might be reframed as, "Are you familiar with the reasons why the initiative two years ago failed? I'd like to hear you talk more about how this project is different."

The question invites the creator to collaborate with the response, rather than defend the idea or battle against the critic. While it does take training, retraining, and personal restraint to abstain from judgment, the benefit is well worth it. Formal feedback sessions should have a facilitator to support both the creator(s) and responder(s) in staying out of their learned negative behaviors.

Respond to Your Voice of Judgment

All well and good, you say, but the judgment of others is the least of my problems—it's the committee in my head that vetoes my best ideas. It may be small consolation to know that you don't suffer alone, but there is hope. One path to relief is to respond to your voice of judgment. Keep track of your internal litany of judgments designed to keep creative energy in check. Write them down. Then write a rebuttal. Or, perform a ritual burning of your judgments and blocks (over the sink, please). Try practicing the same technique that motivational speaker and author, Wayne Dyer, uses when negative thoughts enter his mind: cut them off by saying, "Next!"

Try the technique that has been passed on by creative writing instructors everywhere. Legend has it that John Steinbeck kept a pad of paper next to his typewriter when he was writing *Of Mice and Men*. On it went all of his self-doubts and criticisms: "This is horrible!" "Whoever told you that you could write?" "My editor will have a good laugh reading this chapter!" Listing these internal grumblings temporarily silenced them so he could continue his work until the next judgmental outburst. He patiently gave his committee their "airtime," and then proceeded to write one of the classics of American literature.

Lest you think that easing up on yourself is a private mental health matter with little consequence for others, you are short changing yourself and us beyond words. What if you haven't even begun to tap your creative potential? What if your crazy idea ends up being the seed for the next technological breakthrough, cost-saving measure, or morale-boosting initiative? When your self-centered judgment dams the flow of your originality, we all lose.

Be Fearless

Perhaps the most important attitude you can have in your judge-aholic abstinence is to be fearless. Stripped down to its stinky undergarments, most judgment is just dressed-up fear. (I will echo versions of this theme in almost every chapter.) We lament the lack of innovation and creativity in our lives, yet allow our fear of change, the unknown, surprise, and letting go to get in the way of progress. If your judgment is rooted in fear, you must dig deep into your warrior soul, your Essence, your faith to overcome it. Be without fear. Creation is big enough, hot enough, and generous enough to overcome anything your whiny belief system serves up.

It matters not whether inspiration comes in ideas, images, words, or an eight-year-old's watercolors; they each deserve the time and care to emerge. By practicing *Abstain from Judgment* you create the dynamic field creativity needs to germinate, grow, and flourish.

---

1. Guest, 19.
2. Ray and Myers, 40.
3. Goldberg, 26.
4. "Living Down Expectations," 15.
5. Zemke, 28.

George remembers one of his experiences as a beginning improv student at the Players Workshop in Chicago. "I was in a scene with this woman where we were having a picnic by a campfire. The scene was going along nicely, when all of a sudden the woman got up and said, 'Hey, look at this boat!' and she got in the boat and motioned for me to join her. Well, I had decided that there were many more possibilities with the picnic and the campfire, so I was trying to get her to come back to the picnic. I didn't want to let go. We struggled with this for a while, when our instructor yelled from offstage, 'Just get in the boat!' I had in my mind where the scene was supposed to go, and therefore I was resisting the new discovery. Once I got in the boat, the scene started moving again. That was a very important lesson."

SAY, "YES, AND . . . "

Find Opportunities in Obstacles

| THE PRINCIPLE | How many opportunities have you missed because you chose not to "get in the boat?" Getting in doesn't mean you are going to live there, or sail away for ever and never come back to dry land. You can come back anytime. *Say, "Yes, and . . . ,"* is an invitation to set sail the next time you sit down with your coworker, staff member, team, or boss. You may be surprised and delighted to discover where your journey takes you.

Move the Scene Forward

Say, "Yes, and . . . ," is central to the art of improvisational theater. When improvisers say no to what the moment offers, the creative–collaborative process stops dead in its tracks. The stakes are high in live improvisational theater. A performer only needs to languish on stage once to learn the resistance's power to kill creativity. Are the stakes any lower in your workplace collaborations? Perhaps by placing roadblocks in the way of your colleagues you do not risk humiliation in front of a live audience. You do, however, risk cutting off the vital flow of cocreative energy, missing opportunities for innovation, teambuilding, and even increased profits.

Experienced improvisers know that they must say, "Yes, and . . . ," not only to move the scene forward, but to gain the trust of their fellow players. In their book *Truth in Comedy*, Del Close, Charna Halpern, and Kim "Howard" Johnson say

> *. . . this is a very relaxing way in which to work. A player knows that anything he says on stage will be immediately accepted by his fellow player, and treated as if it were the most scintillating idea ever offered to mankind. His partner then adds on to his idea, and moment by moment, the two of them have created a scene that neither of them had planned.*[1]

When was the last time you described your work collaborations as "relaxing"? You may think it hardly possible. We relax when we know we are in good hands; when we know we will be taken care of and respected. That is not only possible at work, but it is essential if you and your colleagues are going to produce innovative solutions.

In 1997 W. S. "Ozzie" Osborne took over a group engaged in developing a new human interface technology for IBM. "I had just come from the hardware side of IBM, and my programming days had long since passed. But what allowed me to adjust to a new way of operating was trust—in my team and in my gut. When it comes to any learning process, trust is one of the most critical ingredients."[2]

When I take my beginning improv students to their first fully improvised show, they are in awe. The characters and stories seem to evolve so effortlessly, and at times the comedy is so hilarious, the drama so poignant, that it is hard to believe there was no scripting or rehearsing. Back in the classroom the awe wears off as my novice improvisers learn that good improvisation is not about thinking of brilliant lines or assuming peculiar voices. Nor is it about *trying* to be funny, dramatic, or touching. It is simply about having enough trust to get out of the way of the flow, to Say, "Yes, and . . ." to the discoveries and ideas of their fellow players. They discover that the brilliant moments they enjoyed came from accepting whatever is given and adding to it (not necessarily the result of comic genius).

Do not underestimate the power of environment to transform the way you work. Safety and trust are hallmarks of strong creative collaborations. Participants must know that all of their ideas will be listened to ("Yes"), and that they can trust their colleagues to embellish them ("and"). All too often, companies focus on individuals for the success or failure of innovation efforts, and overlook the environment within which they are called to create.

Receive the Gifts

Receptivity to new ideas is the first step on the path to transformation. It is just as important to say "and" as it is to say "Yes." In improvisation circles, we describe each discovery we make and offering we receive from our fellow players as gifts. Our job is to open each gift, marvel at its beauty, and then give something back of equal or greater value. With the power of your gift (your "and"), you can turn every conversation, negotiation, or meeting into a creative collaboration.

Some years ago, I was asked to direct a murder mystery dinner theater show. Though more commercial than my prior work, I agreed. It was a nice break from the long development processes of original theater (and I needed the money). During the rehearsal process, my friend actor Peter Siragusa (who regularly stopped by rehearsals) and I had thought that "we could write something better than this" and went to work on a script. Peter performed at night and I worked days, which left little time to write together. We solved the problem by meeting at a diner near my office to practice saying, "Yes, and . . ." over sandwiches and fries.

We each brought a yellow pad and wrote and talked as fast as we could (I have the ketchup-stained notes to prove it!). We roughed out the entire play and improvised the dialogue by building on each other's ideas. Sometimes the seed idea was less than stellar, but when we added to it, it became something funny, unusual, or surprising. On weekends, we typed and edited our notes. The dinner theater producer loved the script and decided to produce the show. In rehearsals we continued to say, "Yes, and . . ." with the director and cast. While the final script will not be recorded as one of the cornerstones of American theater, it was one of my most refreshing collaborative experiences because it was developed in the spirit of *Say, "Yes, and . . . ,"* and it even enjoyed a year-and-a-half run in downtown Chicago. Had Peter and I resisted the original idea, or labored the collaborative process through dissecting and analyzing each new idea, our show would never have seen the light of day.

I'm not asking you to do anything new. Conscious of it or not, you improvise from the moment you wake up to the moment you drift off to sleep. In large and small ways your life offers you gifts at each turn: an unexpected loss, a new coworker, another software update, a new romantic attraction, a sale on nectarines, a canceled lunch date, etc. In the spirit of *Say, "Yes, and . . ."* each of these is an opportunity. They are nagging inconveniences or the source of great suffering if we choose to fight against them and say no! to the gifts dotting our path.

It is not possible to avoid pain; however, it is possible to avoid suffering. We suffer when we try to wrestle life to the ground and make it behave on our terms. We can live fulfilling, creative lives when we accept what we are given and build on it. Treat life and work as a constant collaboration and you will tap into resources you never imagined you and fellow players had.

Shared Goals

Art unwittingly provided a wonderful opportunity for his children to practice *Say, "Yes, and . . . "* and find their latent creativity:

> *Both of my children have a chore to do each day; but on Saturdays they have a few more than normal. As with most kids, they*

don't like doing chores. I tried something different with them last Saturday and got a nice surprise. When I asked them to do their chores, I gave them the choice to do whichever chores they wanted. They could also complete them their own way. When I returned, I was surprised that they were finished with their chores in less than an hour, because they helped each other to complete the chores. They now do their chores together, because they realize how much quicker they can finish. It dawned on me that I was telling them how I wanted the chores done, and it took them longer and they didn't enjoy it at all. Now they don't mind them at all; plus, they have found out they work well together.

Say, "Yes, and . . ." is a principle of collaboration. Art gave his children an opportunity to *"Yes, and . . ."* by giving them choices. Then they found it was in their best interest to work together—to *Say, "Yes, and . . ."* to each other—in order to attain their shared goal (finishing their chores as soon as possible). What are the shared goals of your collaborations? Might you give them a bit more air, and allow your collaborators to find the most innovative, enjoyable, and perhaps even efficient solution? Like Art's children, successful work teams do two things extremely well: (1) they understand their challenge(s), resources, and expectations (when they say, "Yes" they know what they are saying yes to), and (2) they have plenty of flexibility to find the most innovative solution (they continue to say, "and . . ." until they reach their goal).

A workshop participant recently likened collaboration to an electric circuit. "When we say, 'Yes, and . . .' the circuit is unbroken; all the lights remain on, and no one is left out. No one's contribution is denied or belittled." She was onto something.

Scientists have discovered that at very low temperatures, certain materials have the ability to conduct the flow of electricity with minimal resistance. These materials are called superconductors. The most common conductor of household electricity, copper wire, gets warm due to the resistance that occurs when electrons collide with each other and with copper atoms, resulting in wasted energy. In a superconductor at low temperature, electrons are less likely to collide and the electrons lose less energy to heat, making a highly efficient system for conducting energy.[3]

Just as superconducting materials readily conduct electric energy, we can become superconductors for creativity when we *Say, "Yes, and . . . "*. We energize creativity by removing the obstacles of judgment, control, perfectionism, and many other roadblocks that slow and distort the flow of creative energy. By practicing *Say, "Yes and . . ."* we become a conduit for the flow of what is essentially and completely us.

Levels of Collaboration

Our business relationships, teams, and organizations can be superconductors of collective creativity, as well. When we *Say, "Yes, and . . ."* and abstain from judgment, we remove two key obstacles to the free flow of creativity (control and judgment). Several levels of collaboration become possible: collaboration with ourselves, collaboration with our environment, collaboration with another person, and group collaboration. Each provides opportunities to practice saying, "Yes, and . . . ".

Self-Collaboration. When we work alone, it is easy to forget that we are in a collaborative relationship. "It's all me," we think "I have to rely solely on my own resources!" In fact, when we practice *Listen to Your Essence*, we participate in the most important collaborative relationship of all: a relationship with the source of our creativity. When we listen to this source, accept what we hear, and build on it, our work evolves and we don't get stuck. When we think we're doing it alone, the well sometimes runs dry and we feel as if we have exhausted our resources.

Many successful businesses, my own included, started through self-collaboration. "What if I tried something new?" we heard the quiet voice say. Those who respond with a resounding "Yes!" find themselves on a passionate adventure guided by "and" after "and" after "and."

Environmental Collaboration. When we pay attention, we also collaborate with our environment. A news story, poem, TV repair person, cereal box label, or telemarketing call are all potential gifts to keep our creative energy flowing. Many idea-generation techniques take advantage of these collaborative possibilities. Sometimes playing off a random external metaphor, word, song lyric, object, or article helps you see your challenge in a new light. When you say, "Yes, and . . ." with your desk blotter or a passing cloud (that oddly resembles your Uncle Earl), you provide the conditions for Quantum Creativity. You establish the dynamic gap between yourself (the knower) and your environment (the known). The unexpected will leap from that fertile plane.

One-on-One Collaborations. Creativity loves to play within relationships. Perhaps because they are so familiar, one-on-one collaborations are opportunities easily overlooked. Today we are taught to consider everyone a customer, internally and externally. The challenge of improving customer service is as simple as turning every interaction into collaboration. Deidre, a property manager reports:

> *The principle Say, "Yes, and . . ." helps me a minimum of three to five times a day. And that's on a slow day! In negotiating with existing tenants or listening to their complaints or problems, it's important not to cut them off or say, "That's not going to work" or "That's not the way we've done it." When I throw in the words "Yes, and . . .," somewhere in the first sentence, I can feel the person on the other end of the telephone opening up.*

Deidre discovered the power of *Say, "Yes, and . . ."* to disarm even the most demanding tenant. Concerns over lease terms, maintenance responsibilities, and payment schedules become possibilities for cocreation when Deidre says, "Yes, and let's look for a way to make this work for both of us." The adversary transforms into a partner. And you have transformed the way you work.

Group Collaboration. Whether on a team project at work, planning a vacation, or creating a community mural, we can practice saying, "Yes, and . . ." to tap into the collective resources of the group. Stephen Nachmanovitch says, ". . . inertia, which is often a major block in solitary work, hardly exists at all here: A releases B's energy; B releases A's energy. Information flows and multiplies easily. Learning becomes many-sided, a refreshing and vitalizing force."[4]

Diversity

Saying, "Yes and . . ." not only unleashes collaborative potential, it sends a clear message of mutual respect—something regularly aspired to, but rarely achieved, in business environments. When all members of an organization, from the administrative assistants to the CEO appreciate each other's contributions, the potential for creative collaboration multiplies. Elie Wiesel wrote, "The opposite of intolerance is not tolerance. It is respect." We must do more than "tolerate" our collaborators if we are to reach new heights, and anyway, who wants to be *tolerated*?

Diversity is a popular topic for human resource professionals and trainers. Most corporate initiatives try to raise awareness and sensitivity to differences in culture, race, sexual orientation, religion, and disability. These are noble and important commitments. Awareness is the first step toward action. Saying, "Yes, and . . ." harnesses the abundant diversity of our fellow human beings for creative collaboration. The more diverse the workplace, the more powerful the fuel for creativity. Instead of viewing differences as obstacles, we can acknowledge and accept them (say, "Yes!" to them) and build on the ideas, perspectives, and energy they provide.

Robert Hayles, Ph.D., 1996 President of the American Society for Training and Development, and an international diversity consultant and trainer, says, " 'Yes, and . . .' is something I routinely try to practice when I'm doing diversity training. The use of 'and' is a powerful facilitation tool." Tension arises when we attempt to control the diversity inherent to the creative process, invest in a specific outcome, and see all possibilities contrary to that very specific vision as threats.

In focusing on outward differences in support of diversity, many organizations overlook an often richer source of creativity—inner diversity. By nurturing passion, unique perspectives, and quirky interests, companies can go a long way in replenishing their creative wells. Hallmark Cards liberally supports its writers and artists in exploring new frontiers, sometimes through extended sabbaticals.

Lest you think such luxury is only for the artists, take note of real estate giant, Lend Lease Corporation. Through its Foundation, an employee-managed resource originally endowed through a trust by the corporation, administrative assistants and executives alike regularly receive funding to learn a new language, art form, or even start an exercise program. Other popular programs are Date Night with the family, volunteer outings, and softball tournaments. Recently, the San Francisco region even attended a day at the California Culinary Institute. Nan Cantrell, executive director of the Foundation in the United States says, "From the outside it may look as though we're just giving people money to have fun, but this is serious business. People are gaining important transferable skills and enriching their inner resources. All of that comes back to Lend Lease manyfold." What a wonderful example of alignment! Lend Lease prides itself in finding innovative solutions for its clients and its ability to keep up with rapidly changing business needs. These aren't just words on paper, they are supported with consistent organization-wide behavior. It is true for your organization, and it's true for you: *values supported by action foster integrity.*

When you look for opportunities to collaborate, to *Say, "Yes, and . . ."* you find that the world opens up rather than resists. This is true whether you collaborate with your Essence, the world around you, unexpected life circumstances, individuals, or groups. When you accept and add to the gifts, your creative energy grows and transforms, often into something quite surprising that you would never have imagined had you not been willing to collaborate with your life.

This relaxing, trusting way of working, full of resources and growth opportunities sounds so easy, doesn't it? Yes, and accepting differences and contradictions challenges our comfort zone. Not just us, but pioneering scientists, as well. When physicists discovered that the world does not always act as a machine, they found it quite unsettling. Einstein and other early contributors to quantum theory, challenged the belief that the subatomic world was not deterministic and orderly. Einstein himself declared, "God does not play dice."

Nature is a master of *Say, "Yes, and . . . "*. Today, physicists are working on a unified field theory to make room for the contradictions, explaining gravity, radiation, and the forces in the atom as manifestations of the same force. The wave-particle duality and the inescapable uncertainty of measuring electron location and momentum are only a few such phenomena already mentioned.

The mysterious nature of nature could not be more godlike. The more flexible we become in accepting all possibilities as fuel for the creative fire, the more we celebrate a spirit-filled, enthusiastic life. Before we can join in the revelry, however, we may need to identify still more learned blocks.

| LEARNED BLOCKS |

Only One Right Answer

Wouldn't it be simpler if there really was only one right answer. Roger von Oech, in *A Whack on the Side of the Head*, puts the "one right answer syndrome" on his list of top ten blocks to creativity.[5] We look for one right answer and then stop when we've found *an* answer. The discovery process ends there. We settle in. That's good enough. Lost are all the other possibilities.

Many of us are comfortable with clear-cut answers. It's either this or that; it cannot be both. We were taught from a very early age to perceive the world this way. School taught us that there was one right answer to every question or problem. Our job was to study hard enough (or memorize well enough) to get that one right answer. Our dualistic paradigm was born.

We experience the pain of this paradigm in our personal relationships. How many times have we pursued a point to the bitter end, only for the sake of proving ourselves right? How much pain have we inflicted on ourselves and others for this cause? Years ago a friend shared some words of wisdom with me as I desperately tried to get a loved one to admit she had a drinking problem. I was making us both miserable in the process. My wise friend laid it on the line one day. She said, "Do you want to be right or do you want to be happy?" Saying, "Yes, and . . ." allows us to accept discomfort and uncertainty, and move forward.

Jeffery B. Swartz, president and CEO has led Timberland Company from $156 million to an $862 million global footwear and apparel company. He didn't get there through dictatorship:

> *People have enormous emotional and practical investments in what once worked. . . . As a leader, one of the biggest things I've learned is that I don't always have to be right. I used to feel that the only way to justify my egregious salary was to tell people what to do. I don't let myself do that anymore. Instead, I leave people alone and trust that they'll come up with a suitable solution— and, in turn, that process perpetuates a learning environment.[6]*

At work we may settle for the one right answer for the sake of comfort, routine, or even inertia. In this semidrugged state, we lose the capacity for wonder. Curiosity is an inconvenience left to others who have more time and fewer responsibilities. Is this the life you want? Not just the work, but the life? One right answer limits you to what you know. *Say, "Yes, and . . . "* launches you into the unexplored, uncomfortable, and uncharted. That is a ride you will want to wake up for. So "Get in the boat!"

"Yeahbut . . . "

When we accept all possibilities—even the possibility that there may be more than one right answer—we get out of creativity's way. We respect and support the creative processes of our collaborators, whether clients, colleagues, family members, or friends and allow the creative energy to flow. Not only does this wonderful force flow when we practice this principle; it gathers momentum as each new possibility is added upon the last—unless we say "Yeahbut . . . ." A staple in most Westerners' vocabulary, this word has yet to appear in any dictionary. It is a polite way of denying our own or another person's ideas, impulses, and reality. The impact is not so polite. "Yeahbut" cuts the creative process off at the knees, because it is a form of judgment.

Unlike saying, "Yes, and . . . ," saying "Yeahbut . . ." does not inspire creativity or collaboration. The *yeah* in "Yeahbut . . ." is not the same as the *Yes* in "Yes, and . . . ". Rather than an unconditional acceptance and acknowledgment of the gift, the *Yeah* in "Yeahbut . . ." is closer to "Yeah, yeah, I know all that, but listen to my idea," or, "Yeah, that may sound good, but let me point out the flaws before we take it any further," "Yeahbut, we tried that last year," "Yeahbut, the boss hates purple," "Yeahbut, it's too expensive," Sound familiar?

Expert Mind

Recently one of my students who works in the promotions department for a major soft drink corporation attended a brainstorming meeting for a big event cosponsored by her company. Her immediate supervisor insisted on attending, along with representatives from several other organizations and businesses. "The purpose of the meeting was to get as many ideas out on the table as possible," said Joanne, "but my boss immediately began to criticize and evaluate each one as it was presented. It changed the entire atmosphere of the meeting. We were all very frustrated."

Perhaps Joanne's boss was suffering from a case of expert mind. Knowing too much (or thinking we know everything) can be a formidable block to our creativity. When advertising agencies generate new ideas for product promotions, they regularly bring in staff members from other departments, who have little or no knowledge of the product or its advertising history. I recently facilitated several idea-generation sessions for a large marketing and promotions company. They decided to do things differently by including their operations staff and account executives in the early generation stage. The energy and enthusiasm sparked by this new blood inspired even the most jaded on the creative team. The ideas were fresh, playful, and filled with possibilities. Why hadn't they contributed before? Their response: "No one ever asked us." When the cup of knowledge is full, there is no more room for discoveries, new perspectives, or surprises.

Those who perceive themselves as experts are blocked by the knowledge of what has already been done and by what is considered acceptable practice. Barry Diller, the former chairman of Paramount, Fox, QVC Inc., and current CEO of Silver King Communications, has learned much about expert mind in the trenches of his industry.

> *What all my experiences have had in common is a battle, a holy war if you will, between process and expertise. Expertise is a pack mentality that concludes something can't be done, or that it must be done this way. It's a mentality that relies too heavily on conventional wisdom. It has to. Because the awkward alternative would be to accept that a new thing can't be fully known or comfortably understood. Conventional wisdom, by definition, favors that which has come before, that which is known. That's great if you're building a house or flying a plane. But it's useless, and much worse, dangerously misleading, in creative positions.*[7]

New people in any organization often challenge conventional wisdom. They may be perceived as threats to the status quo. And they often do cause disruptions by enthusiastically questioning the reasons behind procedures and suggesting ways to do things more efficiently or economically. For an organization that is grounded in vision and the spirit of continuous improvement, these fresh troops are invaluable and can, when encouraged, help others see the familiar in a new way.

Objectify Ideas

Unfortunately, many struggle to release their death grip on the status quo, rather than go through the unsettling process of change that can come with doing things differently. One way we learned to maintain that illusion of control was to objectify ideas.

Fear of losing control of or credit for an idea can cause us to put early limits on what the idea can become. While we are trying to establish ownership, the idea or inspiration can become a thing rather than an evolving process. Certain professions may be more susceptible to this block than others; scientists, academics, and artists are only a few whose careers can be built or destroyed based on whether or not they receive proper credit for their work.

While it is certainly proper to acknowledge the source of inspiration, too much vigilance in this direction isolates us from the infinite reservoir of the collaborative process. After a certain point in collaboration, it is folly to try to keep track of what idea came from whose lips, brush, or pen. Not only is documenting the rush of collaborative inspiration unmanageable, but once the collective process has begun, ownership of its fruits truly belongs to the group itself. Person B may have had the idea, but it was inspired by an image from Person A, who was inspired by a phrase from Person C, who was thinking about something his fifth grade teacher said, etc. Without the chaotic Ping-Pong of ideas from collaborator to collaborator, it is unlikely that any one person would have been blessed with inspiration.

Judgment, Control, and Fear

The objectification of ideas may also have roots in the now familiar learned blocks of judgment, control, and fear. Here are three learned responses that served us well in keeping a lid on our creative life energy. It is difficult to say "Yes!" with conviction if we are in the middle of judging our own or another's idea. International corporate trainer Sivasailam Thiagarajan, Ph.D., believes, "If we are worried about whether or not our ideas will work—we won't have any."[8]

George discovered this when he tried to convince his fellow improviser to rejoin him at the picnic rather than go for a boat ride. Initially, he did not see the possibilities of the boat ride, but later reflected:

> We could have sailed to the other side of the lake, met up with pirates, encountered a hurricane, or sailed through a fog and found ourselves in another place and time, but all I could see was how well the picnic was going and thought, 'Why mess with success?'

Premature evaluation similarly narrows the adventures and innovations available to us at work. Brainstorming is one of the oldest tools to support collaborative creativity. The guidelines are simple: any idea goes, one person acts as the scribe, and no one is allowed to judge the ideas, no matter how crazy they sound. Seems simple enough, however, I have seen many brainstorming sessions begin to break down only moments after they've begun. It usually starts with a snicker in response to a crazy idea or a lighthearted jibe at a coworker. Soon people are commenting on each new idea: "We tried that last year and it was a bust," "There's no money in the budget for something like that," "The boss will never go for it." Bam! The judgment boom has been lowered. The censor has been invited into the room. Nonverbal responses can have the same effect as vocal censorship—a frown, a roll of the eyes, a knowing glance across the table to another person. The newcomer (the most valuable player in the collaboration) or the lower-status employee immediately begins to second-guess her ideas. "I haven't been here long enough to say anything," "This might sound stupid. I can't risk my credibility."

This type of censorship is a handy way to protect ourselves from discomfort, from letting go of control. A friend of mine recently had the revelation that all of her character defects, as she calls them, are ultimately rooted in fear:

> *When I am judging others, or trying to control my husband to pick up his clothes, or gossiping about someone, I am really just acting out of my fear. I'm afraid to let go of control, afraid that things won't be OK if I let my guard down or just let people be who they are supposed to be—and that includes letting me be who I'm supposed to be!*

The good news is that we do not need to stay stuck in the darkened room of our learned blocks, we can flip on the light by doing things differently.

| DOING THINGS DIFFERENTLY |

Practice *But* Economics

But is an overused word that should be trotted out only for special occasions. Practice *but* economics. Replace the word *but* with the word *and*, and see what a difference it makes. After I gave a workshop for the American Economic Development Council, I heard a report back from one of the attendees. An upper-level manager (known for his command-and-control style) at a regional utility company had attended along with a handful of his staff. A few weeks later, while chairing a large and somewhat tense meeting, he asked for ideas from the group. As he began responding to an idea, he heard himself say, "Yeahbut . . .". He paused, got a big smile on his face, and amended himself with "Yes, *and* . . .". Upon this his staff initiated a spontaneous ovation that spread to the entire meeting. This man's humility and willingness to do things differently sent a powerful message to the group and released the tension. The meeting came together and solved the problem before them. This is only one of hundreds of examples I have heard and witnessed. Do not underestimate the power of "yes." Of all of the principles I teach, this one has the most immediate and far-reaching impact on organizational culture. Replace *but* with *and* to keep all possibilities alive.

Say It

Just say it. I ask creative teams (and shouldn't every team be creative?) to say, "Yes, and . . ." out loud in idea-generation sessions before they throw their ideas into the hopper. This gives each individual a chance to acknowledge what has gone before and then add to it. Your team will transform the way it works when you transform the way you work.

Beginner's Mind

While you're transforming the way you work, practice beginner's mind. This is the Zen counterpart to expert mind. When we approach life with beginner's mind, we hold an empty cup. There is room for infinite discovery and surprise.

How often have you begun to explore a new area only to discover how much you don't know? This is a common experience among seekers and learners in every discipline. Rather than be overwhelmed by it, embrace it as innocence—a good sign that there is still room in your cup.

Even so, we can be drawn into the glass booth of expert mind where no new discoveries can reach us. How do we restore ourselves to beginner's mind when we have been steeped in an experience or practice for years? Identify the "beginners" in your organization, department, or team. Invite them to join you in the early stages of creative collaboration. They are your most valuable contributors. Open their gifts. Get in their boats.

Another way to resurrect your innocence is to start again from the beginning. Once when I had lunch with a fellow teacher of improvisation, we both found ourselves longing for an opportunity to be beginners again, to have a safe place to fail, and to participate without the scrutiny of thirsty students looking for a demonstration of the "right way" to improvise. As we talked, it occurred to us that we could give that experience to ourselves! We formed a small group of improv teachers and peers and began to meet regularly with no goal other than to enjoy the process and rediscover what we loved so well in the art of improvisation. Each time we meet, I bring my empty cup. It gives me a wonderful opportunity to reclaim beginner's mind and to play.

Play

Play is an attitude. When we adopt it, stakes don't seem so high, and fear of looking foolish drops away. After all, isn't play about being foolish? It is much easier to say, "Yes, and . . . ," when we have not placed life or death, profit or loss, success or failure stakes in the game.

I have heard some of the most innovative ideas called out in the midst of sidesplitting laughter. The space that is created when we allow ourselves to laugh and find humorous connections (which are necessarily the surprising and unexpected ones) is the space we need to allow our deepest inspirations to emerge. The anatomy of humor mirrors the anatomy of innovation. Each requires plenty of room, a lively awareness, a bit of irreverence, and an expectation of delight. The word *humor* was once used to describe bodily fluids whose balance was believed to be a requirement for good health. Physicians have moved on, but the early roots remain an inspiration. A healthy balance of humor in our lives is necessary for good health, as well as innovation.

In the midst of sometimes chaotic idea-generation sessions, I like to support the spirit of play while reinforcing the principles of

Quantum Creativity. Instead of playing the role of disciplinarian, I issue brightly colored "creativity citations" for such violations as tongue clicking, eye rolling, and yeahbut-ing. The fines range from paying a quarter to singing a song. At a recent session, a rather conservative executive was issued the first violation. After sheepishly posing for his Polaroid mug shot, he was mortified to discover that his fine was to sing a song. The entire group cheered and egged him on by starting a round of "Row, Row, Row Your Boat." He joined in and received more cheers and applause. His good humor and willingness to play with the group went a long way in building the community, goodwill, and mutual respect necessary for their success.

Innovation is a living process, not an inert object or singular event. Though the word *play* is most often associated with silliness and recreation, as in *playfulness*, it also means "freedom of motion." To have some play in a fishing line is to have room for the possibility of catching a fish. The space for creation requires both the verb *play* and the noun *play*—action and freedom for action. And, even though "a play" may describe a theatrical presentation, there is no performance here. It is all practice. There is no need to struggle with whether or not to get in the boat. *Say, "Yes and . . ."* gives you the play you need to always contribute to your "play-in-progress."

1. Halpern, Close, and Johnson, 47.
2. Osborne, 98.
3. Lederman, 233.
4. Nachmanovitch, 96.
5. von Oech, 21.
6. Schwartz, 98.
7. Diller, 20.
8. Thiagarajan.

For months my hearty band of actors and visual artists, along with my composer, choreographer, and cowriter meet to develop the theme, characters, and story for our next multimedia production. After two successful productions, my company decides to tackle the subject of "ritual" in Western culture. We throw the net wide as we look for a personal connection to both ancient and contemporary traditions, researching, consulting experts, and drawing on our own varied backgrounds.

After months of workshops, a piece worthy of presentation begins to emerge. We decide it is time to begin the next phase of development and move *Rituals* into production. My collaborators and I start rehearsals, rent a performance space, and set the opening date. One week into rehearsals, obstacles begin to arise. My cowriter feels a life-or-death need to leave immediately for a road trip of unspecified length; the large sanctuary space we rented is not wired for a theatrical lighting system (a fact we discover after our borrowed dimmer board dies a fiery death); we do not raise enough money to cover production expenses; many of the central special effects fail to work; the black-and-white film climax of the show regularly jams in the projector; the highly recommended mask-maker for the pivotal sun goddess character concocts a monstrosity that looks distressingly like an oversized, bright-orange, papier-mâché football helmet; not to mention that in rehearsals the show itself loses the magic we all felt during our earlier playful workshops.

As the director and producer I have many available options: cancel the production entirely, postpone the opening, open it as a work-in-progress, or forge ahead with the full production as originally planned. I choose to do what any seasoned director would—ignore the signs of doom and forge ahead. The looming opening date, the invited press, and all of the invested time and money create in my mind an urgency—a point of no return. Rather than disappoint the friends, family members, and adventurous theater-goers who support us, we open the spirited, but unformed, production.

While directors learn to take both positive and negative notices with a grain of salt, I feel that the headline to our *Chicago Tribune* review is perhaps too kind when it blares: "A Few Funny Bits Fail to Save Awful Rituals." Ouch.

TRUST THE PROCESS

*Discover the Wisdom
of Patience*

| **THE PRINCIPLE** | In the theater our mistakes rarely are private affairs to be quietly swept under the rug. When I gathered the courage to come out of hiding after the show's opening, I realized that I had learned a valuable lesson: I had become so attached to the product that I had abandoned the process. This is like trying to grow tomatoes without tending the soil. The process nourishes the product. Without attention, it will bare anemic fruit, at best.

Though obvious by analogy, business regularly shortchanges the process by focusing only on what can be measured, quantified, and profited from. Without knowing it, you may participate in this creativity-draining practice. The fallout for you and your organization is nothing short of toxic; missed opportunities, low morale, stress, and burnout are a few effects of such misplaced value.

In order to trust the process, you must first work in an environment that is worthy of trust. "Yes, and . . ." collaboration is one of the most powerful ways to cocreate such an environment. It can take some time to build or rebuild trust in a workplace unfriendly to innovation. At the same time, hard-won trust can be destroyed in a heartbeat.

I had an opportunity to consult for a firm conceiving innovative twists for a product they had marketed for many years. They were stuck and needed some help to see the product in a new light. I started by teaching them new ways to work together based on the Quantum Creativity principles. Soon ideas were flying faster than could be recorded. We began to close in on the product assignment for the coming year. During the fourth day of our play together, small groups began to present their concepts-in-progress. Half way into these exciting presentations—complete with song, dance, and visual aids—the CFO walked in and took a seat in the back of the room. Though he remained silent and only somewhat attentive to the presentations, I noticed a change in the breathability of the air. He had informed us that he did not want to disrupt or inhibit the proceedings. And, as is not uncommon, he chose not to attend any of the foundational sessions for the very work he had so heartily supported. Because of his absence, he was not in tune with the spirit of the presentations nor the point in the creative process they reflected.

During the response period for a completely innovative promotions concept, the CFO looked up from his daily planner and asked, "What is the business case for this idea?" After a silence, a brave executive who had participated in all of the sessions tried to explain that the group was not yet evaluating ideas, but fleshing out all of the creative possibilities of the most interesting concepts. "We are not at that stage in the creative process," he replied.

Dryly, the CFO responded "I don't care about your @#!*% process." Translation: "Don't waste my time with your fun and games; tell me about the results!" Uncomfortable chuckles rippled through the room. I tried to salvage the moment with a brief "teaching opportunity" to support all of the time it took to get to this level of enthusiasm and excitement, without pointing a finger at the unwelcome idea killer—the turd now floating in our creative punch bowl.

I was unsuccessful. The damage was done. At the break, one of the participants pulled me aside, "Did you hear that sucking noise?" she whispered. "That was the sound of all of the creative energy being drained from the room." Despite the time and fiscal investment, despite all efforts to the contrary, from that point on all ideas generated for this initiative were evaluated as they emerged. "What would the CFO think?" was always the unspoken criteria. "Can we make a business case for this one?" The process became window dressing to the all-important product.

In this case, though the individuals charged with concept development were quite willing to do things differently, they found themselves bogged down in a culture that did not support them. They quickly reverted to business as usual, not unlike the children or spouse of an alcoholic who try to avert abusive behavior by tiptoeing around or placating the addict. Unfortunately, this kind of dysfunction is by its very nature unpredictable. The dysfunctional system is threatened by any movement toward health and creativity (healthy people cannot be controlled) and will do anything to maintain itself.

Product Obsession

Obsession with the product is the primary means by which business and businesspeople exert innovation-threatening control. It is an illusive malady to root out. Obsession with product is also one of the most difficult hurdles for beginning improvisation students (and young directors) to overcome. When we worry about how we look or if we're being funny and original, we catapult ourselves out of the moment. When we focus on the product or the result of our creativity, we no longer fully participate in the process. This has a profoundly negative impact on the product. We become so invested in a particular outcome that we cut ourselves off from any new possibilities the creative process might present.

We have to relearn this lesson again and again. We promise ourselves we will take time for creativity and passion once that big project is completed, the kids are in school, we finish our degree, the divorce is finalized—all of the time forgetting that the process is the product. After winning the Tony Award for Best Actress, Cherry Jones was asked in an interview how it felt to be called an "overnight success" more than fifteen years into her professional career:

> This reminds me of a story my mother told me. She was taken by her mother—my grandmother—to a revival meeting in middle Tennessee in the early thirties where she was asked, "Little girl, don't you want to be saved?" And she said, "I never knew I was lost." I feel that way about "making it." I feel that every production I've gotten to work on in the last fifteen years has been the greatest experience in the world. I guess in some people's eyes [I] have now made it, but that's not how I look at it."[1]

Take a lesson from Cherry Jones. There is no "making it" in creativity nor in living and working a creative life. There is only the "making." Yes, the making process will generate innovative products, services, and solutions; and the process itself cannot be measured, quantified, or regimented. Like the dynamic quantum field, it is full of potential yet collapses in possibility as soon as it is observed and measured. Demanding quantification or results in the midst of process similarly collapses creative possibility.

Many corporations, eager to encourage creative input have established suggestion systems. One of the most successful is American Airlines' IdeAAs In Action program that regularly saves the company millions through cost-cutting suggestions. Employees are rewarded proportional to the amount of money their suggestions will save the company. Of such systems, the AA program has a number of things going for it, including consistent follow-through guaranteeing employees receive responses to their suggestions within 150 days.[2] Sound good so far? After all, what CFO wouldn't be pleased with those numbers?

Here's the rub: the success of the system is also its liability. By tying rewards to cost-cutting measures, most suggestion systems already limit the innovation potential of their participants. Cost-savings is an outcome—a very specific one, at that. This immediately eliminates suggestions whose cost-benefits are not readily apparent, though they might have significant impact on customer service, brand image, or job satisfaction. Also, cost-cutting ideas are necessarily tied to existing products and procedures—the trap of the causal mechanistic worldview described earlier. By rewarding the outcome rather than participation in the process, most companies make the same mistake I and the I-don't-care-about-your-@#!*%-process-CFO did; they abandon the process for the product, limiting the creative potential for both.

The Japanese *kaizen teian* system provides a wonderful alternative by rewarding participation in the program rather than the outcome of any given suggestion. Here are some numbers that might get your (and your CFO's) attention: In a 1995 comparative study of nationwide participation in United States and Japanese suggestion systems, the average reward for a U.S. suggestion was $458.00, while the average Japanese reward was $3.88. The U.S. worker typically submitted 0.16 ideas per year (roughly one idea for every six workers), while their minimally compensated counterparts submitted 18.5 ideas per year. The difference in participation?: 10.7 percent in the United States, to Japan's healthy 74.3 percent with a 50 percent greater rate of idea adoption.[3]

It's counterintuitive, is it not? The greater the reward, the lower the participation in corporate creativity programs. Perhaps this is not so surprising when you remember your discoveries about passion and your innate motivation for creativity. When the joy of participation is replaced with a reward, there is little left to motivate. Peter Drucker says that in the information age we must manage workers more like volunteers by providing them consistent challenges, opportunities for development, and a belief in the organization's mission.[4] In other words, workers are motivated when given the opportunities to align their personal values and passion with the organization's.

It takes courage to release the death grip on the results of our labor. It also takes patience, according to Barry Diller:

> *Process . . . is ignoring the doomsayers and optimists alike. None of them matters. Process is fundamentally a human function. It can't be duplicated or automated. It's about finding a grain of an idea and following that through to its conclusion. And process can't be forced or rushed. It works for everyone, not just the four or five real geniuses out there.*[5]

This principle of valuing process and letting go of results is at the core of Eastern philosophies. In the *Bhagavad Gita* (one of the Hindu religion's central texts), Lord Krishna counsels the warrior Arjuna, "Pitiful are those who live for the fruits (of action)."[6] If we are motivated solely by our attachment to the product of our creativity, we will never fully express or realize its possibilities; we will be distracted by the transitory and illusory, rather than guided by our Essence.

Attachment limits possibility. Neurophysiologist and cognitive scientist, Francisco Varela, calls attachment to our own ideas and perceptions an "addiction to the self."[7] Just as an obsessive attachment to a substance or process can shut down the natural flow of life energy, so, too, will an attachment to one specific vision or thought shut down the flow of creative energy.

The Living Creative Process

A hand-lettered quotation hangs in the center of my bulletin board above the computer in my office. A friend sent it to me when I was between projects and in one of my earlier mentioned "sensory deprivation periods."

> *There is no meaning with time, no year matters, and ten years are nothing. Being an artist means, not reckoning and counting, but ripening like the tree which does not force its sap and stands confident in the storms of spring without fear that after them may come no summer. It does come.*[8]

—Rainer Marie Rilke

Rilke describes nature's process, as well as the creative process. He speaks universal truth when he instructs the young poet to be patient and trust the cycle of life. Creativity will flow again, ideas will come, the storms will pass and clear the way for summer: "It does come."

The creative process is living and, like all living processes, it is unpredictable, nonlinear, and holistic. We cannot force, control, or contain it, though many have tried. In the midst of writing this very chapter I was called to trust the process. My ideas and words stopped flowing. Struggling did nothing to unloose my thoughts. This chapter needed to "cook" a bit longer. When I (and it) was ready, I returned. The words began to flow again, and I sailed through the sections that once stalled me. (You see, I *did* learn something from my experience with *Rituals*.)

The examples and stories I've shared detail some of the organizational consequences of not trusting the process, along with some very tangible repercussions for you, the individual. You may recognize yourself or your company in this picture. The good news is that when we do trust the process, creativity rehydrates. This is not as easy as this simple principle might suggest. Simple is not always easy. Most of us have spent years doubting, blocking, or otherwise shutting down our intuitive, passionate creative process, or suffering from those whom our creativity threatened. Whether you were victim or perpetrator, hope lies in recognizing your learned blocks.

| LEARNED BLOCKS |

Prescription Creation

I once thought a dose of prescription creation would heal my aching creative process. I was seduced by the past. The mechanistic world-view searches for a formula, a template, road map, a model. "Follow these steps to innovation," it misleads. Do not mistake *Trust the Process* for "trust *a* process." Truly creative acts are by nature unpredictable. Like the illusive wave-particle, it is impossible to determine when or where they will manifest. As soon as the creative process becomes a *thing*, it is no longer alive or able to surprise. Creativity is self-energizing and self-fulfilling; formulas are predictable, consistent, and predetermined.

We get seduced by our need for order. Grahm Wallas first suggested the four stages of the creative process that soon formed the backbone of many problem-solving techniques: (1) preparation, (2) incubation, (3) illumination, and (4) verification. While the evolution of many ideas and concepts naturally follows this sequence (which is what led Wallas to separate the process into stages in the first place), it can be limiting to use it as a prescription for creativity. Such structured processes are sometimes useful in problem solving, which we have seen is a different animal altogether because solutions are necessarily referenced to the defined "problem."

Understand that I am not making sweeping generalizations about all systems and processes. In fact, as you read on, you will hear me sing the praises of boundaries in the service of creativity. I am specifically warning against formulaic approaches to creativity. Our domain is transformation—not simply transformation from one system to another. That would be too easy, and anyway, haven't you been there and done that with the many flavor-of-the-month management models so popular in the past two decades?

The ill-fated production of *Rituals* taught me that what worked in the past will not necessarily work in the present. I approached

the show as I had my two previous successful original productions—
I reduced the organic theater piece to an inert "problem." The initial conditions were consistent with my other original creations, so why not use the same method that brought such rewards before? I mistakenly thought I had found the prescriptive formula for creating original theater. Do you hear the rusty wheels of the machine I constructed grinding to a halt?

I discovered too late that the creative process is not a rash to be cured or a puzzle to be solved. Just as siblings from the same family may need very different kinds of support to thrive, so will each creative opportunity and challenge.

Whether you parent, teach, negotiate business deals, or make art, you must approach each new child, student, business opportunity, or canvas with innocence. Experience need not destroy innocence. Your successes and challenges of the past can guide you, giving you confidence that the path does lead somewhere, even when it takes unexpected turns and presents obstacles.

The End Justifies the Means

Unfortunately, most of us don't enjoy our creative road trips nearly as much as we could. We are more interested in the next rest stop, or impatiently asking the genetically engineered question, "Are we there yet?" We learned the end justifies the means. Though Machiavelli never actually wrote these words, they reflect the essence of his sixteenth-century philosophy of gaining and maintaining power. The product is everything. It doesn't matter how we get there, as long as we get there. This block cuts us off from important discoveries we might make along the way, not to mention from all the fun we might have. When we focus on the product to the exclusion of the process, we abandon the process and ourselves.

The obsessive focus on the product is really no different than an addict's obsession with the fix. We delude ourselves that whatever it takes to get there is worth it, as long as we get there. We raise the

stakes, telling ourselves the product is so important that we are jus-
tified in risking our health, relationships, and even our morality for
it. And the body count can be high. Our ethics may slip, beginning
with innocent white lies, then escalating to full-blown dishonesty.
Our intimate relationships may suffer, professional integrity may
erode, and our personality may change—all in the service of the
coveted goal.

Michele experienced this progression as an art director for a
large advertising agency:

> *When I had those tremendous deadlines, I did whatever it took
> to get the job done. I would work without eating. I would work
> eighty hours a week, or more. I've worked twenty-four hours a
> day, literally without stopping. This was not uncommon. I expe-
> rienced myself as completely detached from my creativity at those
> points and basically just did whatever it took to get the job done.*

Isn't that part of the bargain, you ask? Success stories are filled
with sacrifice and tenacious one-pointed focus on achieving a vision.
Yes, and those who are truly successful are open to discoveries they
make on the path that may lead them in new directions. Vision and
discovery cannot be mutually exclusive. Had Scottish biologist
Alexander Fleming exclusively focused on one result in his study of
bacteria, he would have thrown out the contaminated petri dish he
discovered in his lab. Instead he examined the strange mold and
noticed that it had stopped the growth of the dish's original bacteria. Focusing on the process instead of the product led to the discovery of penicillin!

In Control at All Times

It is not easy to find value in mistakes and to trust the process when
we learned we should be in control at all times. Here is our friend
control again. We were taught to be in control of ourselves, our
emotions, our careers, our relationships, and, ideally, other people

and processes. To not be in control proved failure. Anything less than our original vision of success is a mistake. Lack of passion and motivation for our work means we are lazy. Expressed anger makes us bitches or bastards—unless we cry, then we are wimps. If our careers take unexpected turns, we are losers . . . and on and on.

None of these false beliefs leaves room for other influential forces beyond our control, nor for the fact that no matter how much effort and good intention we put into our work, relationships, and vision, they still unfold in their own time and in their own ways.

Exerting control over a creative process has an insidious way of sucking the life out of it. Linda was an enthusiastic member of a self-directed work team at her company's account service center. Hired in the midst of a reorganization (three regional offices closed and moved to a new central location), Linda hit the ground running with the newly formed team to respond to everything from computer glitches to ordering office furniture. "Within the self-directed work team we were encouraged and allowed to put our heads together to find a solution to our problems. Management trusted our decisions and made us feel valued. People came up with creative solutions and we supported them." So what's the problem, you ask? That's just it, there was none—until a new manager entered the picture:

> *She immediately disbanded the team and chose supervisors in place. Our ideas were no longer sought, we were merely told what to do. As time went on and things were getting ugly, she went back to the teams seeking ideas. None were offered. She tried rewards . . . and still no one cared to expand the effort. . . . The reward of simply working for the common good, which had been sufficient before, was gone—now even bribes, as we saw them, didn't work.*

Are you cringing? The reason for the now empty well seems so obvious from a distance. It is harder to see when you are in the trenches and blinded by your own good intentions. I wonder if we've met.

Be Helpful

I know, I know . . . you were just trying to be helpful. *You* provided all of the resources, set the agenda, rented a lovely off-site location with abundant refreshments, lunch, and two fifteen-minute breaks. You hired me to facilitate your group to solve the predefined problems by 4:15 P.M. (time enough for everyone to rest and change for the poolside cocktail party at 5:30 P.M.). And *I* chose the right collaborators, found the perfect performance space, set the rehearsal schedule and opening date. Ohhhhhh, how I know! After all, we were raised right—to lend a hand, be responsible, keep our promises, carry our own weight (and help others less able). We learned "nice," we learned "helpful"—we learned control.

Helpfulness is just the bright side of control. It looks so good from the outside, but what lurks within is the same old pile of smelly laundry—your agenda, your idea of the right way, your plan. Better go run a load; there's no room for creativity in that.

I can already hear the wheels in your mechanically trained mind turning: "What are you saying? Don't be helpful? What about kindness and compassion? We need more of that in the world, not less!" I couldn't agree with you more, and I am not suggesting that you become the opposite of helpful (which is the only option in a world whose metaphor is a machine). I am asking you to look at your motivation, your relationship to the outcome. There are many ways to be of support without limiting the potential of that being supported. Find them.

Cowardice

When we are compelled to control, we may mask a deeper affliction: cowardice. I originally named this block "fear." It sounded so much more noble than "cowardice." Cowardice connotes weakness of character—who wants *that* title? So, in an uncharacteristic attempt at manipulation, I name this block cowardice hoping to reach the ten-year-old child in you who, in response to such name-calling, puffs out his chest and says, "Who are you calling a coward? I'm not afraid—just watch me!" Perhaps this will provide an opportunity to look at your fears in a new way and discover which ones are truly useful for your well-being and which hold you back.

When I ask clients to name creative blocks, fear is usually at the top of the list: Fear of failure, fear of looking stupid, even fear of success. All are ultimately rooted in a fear of losing control, a fear of letting go. The irony is that when we stop and look at the reality of our experience, try as we might we can't control other people, places, things or processes. We can't even control our own creative process. So to you long-suffering "control freaks," I say, "Let go, you coward! And try . . . doing things differently."

| DOING THINGS DIFFERENTLY |

Ask for the Tea

Sit down, relax, and ask for the cup of tea. Bruce Jordan, the director and producer of the long-running murder mystery *Shear Madness*, often used a story about legendary actors Alfred Lunt and Lynn Fontaine to remind his actors to keep their performances fresh night after night, month after month. Lunt and Fontaine, noted for their perfectionism, were nearing the end of a successful run of a show. Alfred Lunt was frustrated. "I can't understand it!" he blurted out. "I always used to get a laugh in that scene when I asked for a cup of tea. What's wrong?" "Well," mused Fontaine, "Perhaps you should go back to asking for the tea instead of for a laugh."

When we embrace the process, the product takes care of itself. This does not mean that we lack vision, but that the vision serves as a guiding force rather than a straitjacket. Focusing on the product often destroys the lively vision that we sought in the first place.

Water Your Relationships

At work, as elsewhere, the process often lives in interactions; it happens *between* living organisms. So, water your relationships. Nurture your relationships with colleagues and clients as would a loving gardener. Attend them, and give them plenty of sunlight and air.

I am surprised when some managers think that they don't want their employees to be creative. True, you don't want your insurance adjuster, bank teller, or pharmacist experimenting with your numbers or dosages. You do, however, want them to listen, understand your needs, and respond to those needs quickly. Improvisation is about relationships. Without the magnetic, unpredictable interplay of human upon human, with one adding to the contribution of the other, nothing compelling is created.

Relationship selling has taught us not to go after the sale (the product), but to build the relationship (the process). That's more interesting anyway, isn't it? An improviser is already in trouble if she begins a scene with an idea of where it should go. No longer is she playing in the moment and trusting her fellow players to give her valuable gifts. She has abandoned the process in an effort to fulfill her personal agenda. Customers are the same way; they tend to turn into so many rock formations when you have decided for them what they need and when. But show up for the relationship, and see them come to life!

Does this still sound a bit touchy-feely to you? You don't have time for this; you've got to make your numbers. That's all your boss cares about. It's what you get paid for. Perhaps you are again stuck in the old either-or way of thinking. A former student discovered how to have her financial cake and eat it, too; in fact, it wouldn't have worked any other way:

> *At my new job my objective is to acquire almost one million dollars in cost savings for our company. After meeting with my customers—one being our maintenance department—I thought it*

was going to be impossible. My new peers are very aggressive and abrupt, but this is not my style. By making friends with my maintenance customers and really listening to them, I've earned their trust, and together we are able to get some of these savings. I cannot just tell a department that they have to do things our way; but, by being patient, they are seeing it themselves. By focusing on the relationships rather than the product, the product is happening naturally, easily, and most important (to me), jointly.

Think of relationships as the illusive quantum field from which all possibilities spring. You cannot measure them or even see them sometimes, and without them nothing will emerge. Literally, no *matter*.

Surrender

Sometimes we need our wake-up calls in big bold letters. Envision the Wicked Witch of the West writing this message across the sky to you: Surrender, Dorothy! Even then, you may be hit with a sudden attack of blindness or convince yourself that this particular message is really intended for someone else, or, if it is for you, surely it is intended for another, less chaotic time than this! Certainly there will come a time when you can spend hours in meditation and take long walks in the woods. Surely such messages are meant for times like that—not now, when you have deadlines to meet, children to raise, social obligations to attend, laundry to do, and then there is that fundraiser to organize. Surely, not now!

Of course, when life is at its highest pitch, we have to surrender. We hit bottom, realizing that trying to control all of the converging processes makes everything worse, not better. In response, we throw up our hands, "That's it. I give up! I just can't do any more!" And occasionally, we have the presence of mind and spirit to surrender well before we lose ourselves in the sometimes raging rivers of life.

I have many opportunities to surrender these days. In the early days of following my current passion, I spoke to organizations or designed a seminar for a company once every few months. This provided a nice balance to my teaching, writing, and directing. I planned weeks, sometimes months, in advance—researching, outlining, preparing handouts and slides, rehearsing, rehearsing, and rehearsing. As my presentation day drew near, I focused my energy. I let friends and family know I would not be available until after the event was over. Upon its completion, I let out a big sigh of relief, gave myself a few days off, and began to focus on the next event looming on the horizon.

Due to increasing demands, today I do not have time for such obsessive preparation. Of course, I still prepare. What has changed is my relationship to the process. I now (or more often than not) surrender, and trust that, though I am responsible, I am not ultimately in charge. In this new relationship, sometimes the most interesting connections emerge. There is actually room for the audience (and me) to transform in response to our shared experience; there is space for quantum leaps.

Surrendering is not a one-shot deal. You may need to do it two hundred times each day. The good news is that you do not need your own private woods or beachfront property to find the serenity necessary to trust the process; the opportunity is there in chaos and calm alike.

Don't Think About It

It also helps if you don't think about it. Many experience life on an intellectual level, even if we do not fancy ourselves as intellectuals. We analyze, theorize, and philosophize until we are paralyzed. While this may give us an illusion of control, it is ultimately debilitating.

Thinking can annihilate trust. The improviser does not pause to plan what to do when he sees a fellow player faltering in a scene, he just leaps in trusting that he will have a gift to offer. You, too, will discover your gifts when you jump in with the singular intention of making a positive contribution. Note: The intention to "save the day" or "solve the problem" will disable you. Such intentions pressure you to come up with a result. Your job is to bring a gift (anything—even a yo-yo, paper cup, or houseplant) to keep the party going, and to trust that others will bare their riches, too.

When you listen to your essence and follow your passion, the mystery unfolds. Had I done a little less thinking and a little more being during the production of *Rituals*, I might have noticed that the process was trying to tell me something. I simply chose not to listen.

By claiming responsibility for our experience, we claim our "respond-ability." Next time, we may even choose to do things differently.

---

1. Jones, Cherry *Equity News*, 4.
2. Robinson and Stern, 146.
3. ibid, 63.
4. Drucker, 21.
5. Diller, 20.
6. Yogi, 138.
7. *Crisis of Perception: Art Meets Science and Spirituality in a Changing Economy*, Video.
8. Rilke, 30.

One hundred days to train 60,000 employees worldwide on a brand-new auditing system. Little more than three months to get auditors from two once separate companies with differing corporate cultures to let go of their familiar ways of working and start doing things differently. This was just one of the challenges for the newly merged Pricewaterhouse Coopers. The company had to put the new audit system in place before the busy audit season, resolve software and hardware conflicts, reorganize and physically move service areas into new offices, and complete leadership transitions. Sound like chaos? It was. Chaos filled with opportunity and growth. Rather than leaving a legacy of bruised egos, frustrated and demoralized employees, and other human and emotional carnage, PricewaterhouseCoopers effectively harnessed the power of chaos for positive transformation.

Chicago Managing Partner William Bax attributes the success to clear vision and positive attitudes, "We believe in articulating our values and backing them up with positive action. Yes, we had to create and implement a new methodology in a short time period. But when everyone knew that they were part of the plan, they jumped into the fray. New teams worked together as if they'd done so for years. As we worked to achieve a shared vision, the high-velocity change fueled our success, rather than derailing us."

EMBRACE CHAOS

Learn Nature's Lessons in Creativity

| **THE PRINCIPLE** | *Embrace Chaos* often elicits uncomfortable chuckles when I first present it to businesspeople. However, when they realize that some of the biggest breakthroughs in science and industry, as well as positive organizational transformations and individual growth, cannot happen without chaos, they pay attention. PricewaterhouseCoopers reaped benefits from chaos far beyond improved bottom lines. They emerged with a stronger vision, culture, and employee commitment than ever before. Bax relays additional benefits, "We have an even larger presence in the community now and are recognized as a firm that is an important part of the city's social fabric. We look forward to having a positive impact here."

Within the apparent randomness of chaos lies infinite opportunity. Scientists now understand that natural systems use chaos, or what looks like chaos, to reach a higher level of order. When necessary chaos is interrupted, the system breaks down. In Greek mythology, Chaos, from which modern chaos theory draws its name, was a dynamic, random state from which all of life emerged. This state eventually organized itself into to a gigantic egg, which then gave birth to Heaven, Earth, and Eros (the god of love). The myth is consistent with science and again strengthens the analogy for creativity. Both myth and science describe a dynamic void from which all possibilities manifest.

Life is change. This is not a metaphor. If we are not changing or experiencing change, we are not living. This chapter will help you develop the flexibility to find opportunity in chaos. Management pundits, CEOs, and headhunters all join in the chorus asking for workers who are able to thrive in a climate of constant change. If you can, you are worth your weight in stock options.

Persistent Instability

Though chaos is largely a mathematical science, as an analogy it illuminates the creative process. Two of the most important (and paradoxical) aspects of chaos are: persistent instability (constant, unpredictable change) and self-organization (integrity maintained in the midst of change). Both characteristics are reflected in creativity expressed in the arts, business, technology, and even in your personal life.

We all experience "unorganized states," wasting much energy battling them, and missing the growth they invite. Michael remembers his experience as a child, moving to a new school in a new neighborhood, always being an outsider, never quite fitting in. "I hated school and I was always getting in trouble." There was a turning point, though. While many memories have faded, Michael remembers every detail of his fourth-grade geometry class and teacher.

I sat in the front row and, instead of paying attention to the teacher, I was in my own little world. I made paper airplanes during the entire class. Rather than discipline me, my teacher, Mrs. Rubenstein, saw a doorway into my little world, and instead of trying to shut me down and make me behave in the "right" way, she used my interest in airplanes as a way to get me excited about learning. She used the angles in my planes to teach me about triangles and other concepts in geometry. It was the first time anyone really appreciated my interests. It really opened me up to learning.

Rather than succumb to an illusion of control (a notion seasoned teachers will agree is just that—an illusion), Ms. Rubenstein embraced chaos and her nonconforming student, making room for a life-changing learning experience. Not only did she guide her student to a passion for geometry, she inspired him to be a lifelong learner. Today Michael is finishing his master's degree and working as a community activist providing computer training in a successful welfare-to-work program. Thank you, Ms. Rubenstein. Thank you, chaos.

Chaos is persistent instability.[1] Newtonian physics tells us that if we know all of the variables of a system at one point in time, as well as forces acting on the system through time, we can later predict its behavior. When the initial conditions cannot be completely known, it becomes impossible to make accurate predictions about a system. It is possible, however, to see patterns of behavior in the system as a whole, which tells us certain self-organizing principles are at work. The weather, population growth, and the stock market are a few examples of such chaotic systems.

Self-Organization

The persistent instability of chaos gets more PR and often engages our energy so completely that its self-organization eludes us. Understanding the larger picture can give you the tools and inspiration to use chaos to transform the way you work.

Scientists use the term *feedback* to describe fluctuations in chaotic systems such as fish populations. Feedback regulates the system and keeps it from losing integrity. In an isolated pond with abundant food and without predators, fish populations grow quickly. At a certain point they become so large that there is no longer enough food to go around. This provides the natural feedback to the population growth, which soon begins to decrease in response to the food shortage.[2] The same happens in processes ranging from gas prices to the human heartbeat; the system reaches a point of maximum expansion or effort and then it contracts. This is what is meant by a self-organizing system. Some systems reach a new equilibrium altogether without returning to the previous state. There is no need to control this process, because it naturally regulates itself.

Rather than look at these fluctuations as signs of system breakdown, scientists now see them as part of systemic evolution and necessary to the system's well-being. Ary Goldberger at Harvard Medical School found that the heart rhythms of healthy patients are, in fact, more chaotic than those of heart-attack patients. He concluded that "chaos gives the human body the flexibility to respond to different kinds of stimuli. . . ."[3]

In a self-organizing system the events and fluctuations that challenge the status quo are, in fact, the most useful to its evolution. In this light, the unexpected is not something to overcome, but the most important part of the process. Although chaos is by definition unpredictable, experts in organizational development and adult learning agree that little transformation occurs without chaos' ingredients.

Any system that cannot "hear" or respond to feedback presents symptoms of progressed stasis. Amory Lovins, cofounder and vice president and director of research at the Rocky Mountain Institute, offers

> *Big hierarchical companies in general are neither fast nor smart*
> *. . . . The bigger you get, the more difficult it becomes to main-*
> *tain effective feedback systems. And systems without feedback are*
> *stupid, by definition.*[4]

It is all too easy to wag a blaming finger at the hulking system—
to blame the "other." It's easy, and it won't do you a bit of good. It
won't help you transform the way you work. Recognizing yourself
as a system (and part of a system) will. Learning to listen to your
feedback will.

Strange Attractor

As you chart your way through career changes, technology devel-
opments, market fluctuations, or even a typical day filled with events
beyond your control, take heart that a larger organizing process is
at work (pun intended). Scientists David Ruelle and Floris Tokens
made graphs to describe how systems evolve over time. A chaotic
system does not settle into a repeating pattern. But in the very long
term it converges to a pattern, nonetheless, called a "strange attractor." "Strange" because the pattern is not familiar, and "attractor"
because the trajectories of the system get closer and closer to a pattern. Chaotic systems allow wide randomness and play, but the system holds together. No two snowflakes are alike, but they are all
snowflakes. The boundaries provided by nature allow systems to be
locally changing while globally stable.

Successful businesses create similar boundaries to direct their
growth. Individuals and organizations with a strong vision fare
much better on the sea of change than those without. For example,
individuals and businesses that focus only on profit (perhaps choos-
ing a career because it is hot, or responding to an immediate financial opportunity) without a larger mission, regularly find themselves
directionless when real storms hit. Such was the case of a once thriving Chicago theater company that began to fade off the map in the

early 1990s. The headline in the local paper aptly described the cause of the company's demise as "The Sins of No-Mission."

I put that lesson to work on a Colorado business retreat some years back by developing a mission statement for my company that lights my way to this day. It reads simply: To emancipate the creative spirit. This vision provides stability even in the shifting sands of my consulting, speaking, writing, and teaching. I know to stay my course (because I have one) during times of great change, and not to seize ill-fitting, but temporarily rewarding, offers (such as the time I turned down a lucrative opportunity to learn and present another company's team-building seminars). Let your vision be your guide. One day you will step back and see the beautiful, if strange, patterns in your own chaotic life.

Ride Change

You can develop the flexibility and stamina to respond to chaos by becoming fluent in the language of the creative process. The self-organizing power of natural systems teaches us much about the sometimes unpredictable nature of life. Looking at the small (locally changing) picture it is difficult to find meaning (global stability) in our daily challenges, setbacks, or even in our triumphs.

No matter your business, everyday you are called to respond to change. In the perhaps mythical past (against which we seem compelled to compare our current challenges) it may have worked to "ride out" change, as one would wait out a passing squall. You reasoned that when things settled down you could get back to business as usual. After all, radical instability was not a common occurrence (at least that's how we remember it).

You don't have that kind of luxury today. There is no riding out, hunkering down, or heading for cover. It's business as *un*usual, or you aren't in business at all. Just ask the folks at a large credit card management company. After a number of mergers, reorganizations, and a recent buyout, they have had to learn the language of change. One executive reflected, "Success begins and ends with flexibility. You won't get anywhere fighting change. If you go in with an attitude that you might actually learn something, that there may be a better way to do things, you will always find the opportunities." No, riding out change is no longer an option. Riding its waves is. Surf's up—grab your board and you will have the time of your life!

And what a time it is! Just when you find your balance—bam! Another wave knocks you into the drink. Perhaps you find yourself reorganized into a new job (or out of one altogether), become ill (or are called to care for someone who is), or find an important relationship in transition. In the moment, it is difficult to appreciate the value of such chaos with all of its emotional, physical, and spiritual turmoil.

On the other side of these difficult periods, we often appreciate their value. We gain new insights or see that, though we would never have planned the events that took place, they led us to exactly where we needed to be. In fact, the chaos was crucial to reach our own higher level of order. Yes, without these AFGOS (another friggin' growth opportunity, as a friend calls them) you wouldn't be who you are today. And, you have to admit, that's pretty wonderful.

Margaret Wheatley and Myron Kellner-Rogers describe the necessity of life's chaotic "messes":

> *Life uses messes to get to well-ordered solutions. Life doesn't seem to share our desires for efficiency or neatness. It uses redundancy, fuzziness, dense webs of relationships, and unending trials and errors to find what works.*[5]

Those messes that we want to avoid, control, or deny are exactly the stuff from which life and growth emerge. Chaos stirs up our pot and gives us new information, combinations, and options that we cannot see when all of the "good stuff" is settled at the bottom.

Emma shared her story of a series of unexpected, and initially unwelcome, messes in her life. After several years of enjoying what she experienced as a solid marriage, her husband came home from work one night and said, "We need to talk." Emma reported,

> *I was rather excited because I thought we had needed to talk for some time but was never able to get him to participate. We sat in the living room and in a matter of maybe two minutes, he said he no longer loved me; he no longer wanted to be married; and he had seen a lawyer and filed for divorce. I was speechless. I could not even react.*

Despite her attempts to find an alternative, the divorce went through. Not long afterward, Emma's company closed the local office and asked her to leave the only community she had ever known and relocate to Chicago. Though this brought more loss to accept, this time she welcomed the change.

> *The timing was perfect; nothing was holding me back. As a result of the events of my divorce and recovery, so to speak, I feel I have become a very different person. I have tried to learn from my mistakes, rather than become bitter or overly cautious as a result of them. I have continued my education and developed my career to a greater level than I ever imagined possible. And I no longer set limitations for myself. If I think it's worth pursuing, I pursue.*

Emma found the opportunities in apparent chaos. The radical change provided the feedback that took her to a new level of fulfillment. Had she battled the unexpected (and inevitable), she would have missed the opportunities; she would have interrupted the natural flow of her life process.

Integral Chaos

Chaos is as integral to the creation of art as it is to your life and work. In creating new shows, I have found that chaos often emerges midway into the development process. Everything my collaborators and I thought we knew about our vision of the show becomes fuzzy, and we go through a period of seemingly knowing less than when we started. When we continue to participate in the process and make new discoveries, we move through the fog into greater clarity. Soon the piece presents itself to us again, richer and more fully formed than ever before.

Despite the number of times I have experienced chaos during the creative process, I still sometimes have a knee-jerk (and, I believe, learned) response of fear and a desire to control. "This will be the one time things won't work out," I tell myself, "Maybe I should sit down and 'figure out' where we went 'wrong' and get this thing back on track." Fortunately, except for the notable exception of *Rituals* described earlier, these have been fleeting impulses. I soon remember that I have been here before and if I trust the process and the shared vision, our creation will move through these crucial "growing pains" to reveal its full potential.

Don't obstacles make the story more interesting, anyway? We are brought to the edge of our seats as we watch the characters meet and overcome their challenges. The closer they come to failure before escaping what appears to be certain doom, the more engaged we are. It's not the obstacles themselves that intrigue us, but the excitement of watching others overcome them and participation in the triumph and wisdom that comes with victory. After all, what good is moving through chaos if we do not learn anything from our trials, if it does not take us to new heights? Embrace chaos and your life needn't be an imitation of art—it will *be* art.

Chaos is often a catalyst for building community, as well. In response to a crisis, whether a company-wide change or an unexpected problem affecting a family, people often come together for mutual support. When the vision or greater good is clear, as it was during the PricewaterhouseCoopers merger, the self-organizing factors are in place. Clive Newton, PricewaterhouseCoopers global leader of human resources says, "It's clear that success in the twenty-first century is going to require additional values, such as speed and innovation. . . . They must serve us through major—and unpredictable—change in our businesses and the marketplace." The stories that touch us are those of extraordinary character drawn out during such crisis. By embracing chaos together, long-lasting bonds are formed, making the framework of a true community, one that is able to commune.

If you are tempted to dismiss the glowing reports of productive chaos at PricewaterhouseCoopers as the comments of out-of-touch upper-management, or the PR version of the merger, read the representative comments of people I interviewed on the front lines:

"I've never met a more cooperative group—everyone wanted it to work."

"I can't think of a better place to work."

"I love it and the challenge that goes with it."

With this kind of relationship to change in a highly collaborative environment, PricewaterhouseCoopers met its 30 percent growth goal in the merger year. Its employee retention numbers also bested the national merger retention average by 4 percent, particularly worth noting in today's sellers-market job climate.

With all of the opportunities in chaos, we ought to welcome it. Most of us, however, have lost our fluency in the language of change and flexibility to respond to opportunities in chaos. Instead of embracing chaos, we brace for chaos. Yet again, we may have picked up some learned blocks.

| LEARNED BLOCKS |

Disorder Is Bad

The blocks that taught us not to trust the process also cut us off from taking advantage of chaos's power. They are fear and illusion of control. In addition, we learned disorder is bad. When things get out of control, it is our job to get them back on track—the sooner the better, or we will all suffer. After all, our credibility, reputation, and maybe even our job are on the line. At least, that is what we believe. Unfortunately, these are the false beliefs of the mechanistic paradigm, which values order, predictability, and efficiency above innovation.

Steve Brewton from Motorola's Advanced Product Division was charged with improving quality in his product group in an unprecedented eight-week window. His team of engineers was given wide latitude to do whatever it took to meet this goal. "My explicit instructions were that our management group was to remove any obstacles we encountered; we had no limits." With that, Steve and his team set to work using a brainstorming technique that ensured maximum participation and minimum judgment. The team moved quickly to implement the system that grew out of their collaborative effort.

The initial results were startling. Despite comprehensive improvement strategies, the results showed product quality actually getting worse. This did not deter the team's efforts; they had a larger vision in mind and trusted that they were headed in the right direction. The second reporting cycle showed marked improvement—improvement so successful that the first full quarter following the initiative produced a nearly defect-free product line. Had Steve and his group responded to the initial disorder as a sign of failure, or adjusted in response to short-term chaos, they would have aborted the now legendary success of their collaboration.

Nature teaches us to embrace disorder. Unpredictability does not equate failure. Disorder is a gift—a sure sign that life is present and the process is evolving. If, out of fear, we step in to take control, we cut short the evolution, we return to the familiar, we curtail possibilities. When we try to force order out of chaos, we do so according to our past experience, knowledge, and preconceptions, thereby limiting creation.

Chaos Wastes Time

Sometimes our efforts to reestablish order are fueled by the belief that chaos wastes time. I often wonder where the idea that time could be "wasted" took root. If ever there was a concept born of perception, this is it. "Wasting time" implies that certain activities and ways of being are inherently more valuable than others. If you clean out the garage or revise the department's budget, you are not wasting time. If you stare off into space or browse in the corner bookstore, you are. This principle challenges our most basic assumptions about our purpose on the planet.

Yes, embracing chaos may take longer than taking control (though as many examples in nature and business refute as support this assumption), just as it may take longer to get the entire company's support of a new mission statement or the family's agreement on vacation plans. The result of inviting participation—respect, harmony, and happiness—is well worth the time and, in the long run, consumes far less energy than if the natural process of the system, organization, or creation is not honored. If we value participation, collaboration, and creativity, embracing chaos will never be a waste of time.

We may be surprised at how quickly the creative process evolves when we embrace chaos. Sometimes the route is much faster than we ever imagined. Unquestionably, nature's process will be more efficient than the time we spend cleaning up the messes that result from a fear-based need to control.

Chaos as Unproductive

Still, we may justify our actions with another learned block, that chaos is not productive. In nature, chaos is not only productive, it is essential to production. With each swing of the pendulum, the system evolves. When these swings are artificially controlled, growth is limited. When we focus on the end result or one rigid vision, we miss one of the most valuable products: insight. Jeff shared this story of an experience that led him to just such a revelation:

It was the first time that I met my fiancée's parents. Her father is a very upright, successful businessman who is the president of a medium-sized company. Upon our first meeting we did what was the proper thing to do—go to the country club for a round of golf while my wife and her mom hung out poolside. Going to play golf with my future father-in-law made me a little nervous, but I had confidence in myself, because I was a pretty fair golfer. On about the fifth hole I happened to hook my tee shot into the rough. When we drove to the area where we thought the ball was, we discovered that it had landed fifteen feet in front of a huge tree. After spotting the ball and realizing that I had absolutely no shot at the green, I uttered the words, "Oh shit." At that moment, "Big Jim," as I like to call him, looked me straight in the eye and remarked in his Southern accent, "Jeff, that there is not a problem—that's an opportunity." For some reason it was like lightning striking me from above. At that moment I realized, "You know, he's right. Let's make the best of this situation." I proceeded to take out my five iron, approach the ball and intentionally hook it in a fashion that gave me a shot that landed on the green. Never would I have imagined that such a "miracle shot" would get me on the green. If my tee shot had landed right in the center of the fairway, I would almost bet that out of ten tries on my approach shot, none of them would have equaled my "miracle shot." The lesson learned that day taught me to accept the unexpected with open arms.

Chaos—Sign of Weakness?

Jeff found the opportunity in chaos and in doing so, also overcame the learned belief that chaos is a sign of weakness. This is a block I hear most often from businesspeople. If things are "out of control," it must be the result of someone's incompetence—because competent people are "in control." This block is difficult to overcome; it involves letting go of the judgments from others, as well as our own learned beliefs. The truly competent possess the wisdom of the process and the courage to let it have the freedom to reach its full potential. Just as too much control stifles a child, it will mute creative possibilities.

Too often when managers express disappointment in the quality of ideas generated, they blame the people charged with the creative responsibility, rather than look at the work environment. They neglect to ask if the full spectrum of the creative process was supported, or only the end result? Are ideas welcomed from any source within (and without) the organization? Do all employees know that their ideas will be given attention, and implemented if they are viable improvements? These are just a few crucial characteristics of a work culture that supports lively awareness (and implementation) of possibilities. When results of business creativity initiatives disappoint, it is rarely a sign of individual shortcoming, but a call for organizational growth.

Fear of Loss

For some, organizational growth presents a painful catch-22. Growth means change. Change means letting go of what was. So the final barricade to practicing *Embrace Chaos* is fear of loss. Chaos often brings along the threat of losing something to which we are dearly attached. Fear of losing our original vision for an idea, status, or even a job can flip us into a control mode that suffocates creation. True, creation brings destruction. To move forward, or to move at all, something is left behind, destroyed, made obsolete. Disposable diapers left much of the baby pin industry behind; cell phones made an 18 percent dent in pay-phone revenue in 1999; and when was the last time you heard the sound of a typewriter in your office? Dwelling in loss only enervates creativity, making it impossible for the ashes to give rise to the phoenix.

In the midst of chaos we cannot see what lies beyond the possibility of loss—more abundance and growth than we ever thought possible. Moving through the pain of loss has no substitute. If we choose not to let go in order to elude pain, we subdue creativity and miss opportunities. Creativity thrives in abundance. When we release our death grip on what is, we make room for what will be. We make room for doing things differently.

| DOING THINGS DIFFERENTLY |

Be Accident-Prone

During a 1990 interview on *Good Morning America*, Billy Joel said he tries to be accident-prone when composing: "The only thing truly original is a mistake." Joel was talking about chaos, and he knows how to use it. "Accidents" and "mistakes" are matters of perception. They can be obstacles or opportunities.

The chemistry for Scotchgard brand fabric protection, aspartame sweetener, and the technology for ink-jet printers were all discovered by accident. Each of these apparent mistakes, however, could have easily been overlooked. For each to be realized, it took the alchemy of individuals who saw possibilities in the unexpected and work environments that supported continued exploration. G. D. Searle and Co. was a pharmaceutical company pursuing a new antiulcer drug when a lab assistant discovered that one of the drug's components had an extraordinarily sweet taste (a fact he discovered when he licked his finger hours afterward). This discovery was almost not pursued—it wouldn't have been had the company been unwilling to let go of its sole focus on pharmaceuticals.[6] Monsanto's NutraSweet company spawned by this discovery has made millions from seeing the possibility in an accident.

Our lives are also full of such uncomfortable accidents. Unexpected discoveries, radical changes, and crises can catapult us into the here and now. These wake-up calls can lead us back to ourselves, our Essence. One day we are going about our routine—feeding the cat, blow-drying our hair, catching the bus to work. The next day everything has changed. The street we walked hundreds of times before now seems foreign, the once habitual business of the day is awkward, and what we once found comfortable now refuses to console.

A friend told how her experience of her apartment changed after she and her partner broke up. "What was once the cozy home I looked forward to coming to at the end of the day, became a place where I had to be with a lot of difficult feelings." This "accident" led her to a new relationship with herself. Looking back on the year after the breakup, she reflected, "It was one of the hardest years of my life, and one of the best."

Have an Open Hand

My friend, along with many others, learned to embrace chaos by approaching life with an open hand. Release your grip. If you need to hold on to something to keep it, it never belonged to you in the first place. An open hand is a reminder to let go of control in many areas of life including work, family, relationships, and artistic projects. Let the sands of your life flow through your fingers; the breeze of possibility blow through your soul.

Lighten Up

There are always more challenges from where they came from, so lighten up. Surely you've heard how to make God laugh—tell him your plans! The joke is on us, isn't it? Sometimes the best response when things don't go as we planned is laughter. If we cannot laugh now, our humor will be restored later. When we step back, we see what a great sense of humor the universe has. It gently reminds us that we are not at its center.

Much anger, resentment, and frustration comes from a mistaken belief that things are supposed to go perfectly—that we were supposed to have a wonderful childhood, get into the college of our choice (or go to college at all), meet the perfect mate, find the perfect job, work for a perfect boss, and generally have a seamless, linear, perfect life. When we let go of this illusion and of the belief that we are somehow owed an apology for all of our disappointments (from whomever is handing out apologies these days), we can get on with life and maybe even have time to listen to the feedback.

Listen to the Feedback

It's no coincidence that I was delivered a made-to-order opportunity to embrace chaos while writing this chapter. I was truly called to practice what I preach when I returned from a business trip to find that the ceiling above my office computer had collapsed from a water leak. The hard drive was damaged beyond repair. I soon found myself in the midst of debris removal, insurance negotiations, new product research, setting up and learning a new system, and resurrecting data—all while designing a client's new innovation program and consulting several hours each week out of the office (besides preparing for the holidays and family visits).

The "new improved" system was filled with bugs and software conflicts causing frequent freezes and crashes. What would ultimately be an upgrade required a significant investment of time and money to run smoothly. Once I found my way back to my sense of humor, I could enjoy the irony and evolution propelled by the chaos. My obstacles provided just the feedback I needed to leap to the next level in my business and personal growth, just as a stressed natural system uses such feedback to self-organize.

Here are just a few of the gifts I received once I was able to embrace chaos. I found resources I never knew were available. I now have a list of consultants, help-line numbers, and on-line support options. This resource-gathering mission led me to hire another part-time staff person, freeing me to better serve my clients. I learned more about downloading, hot-booting, and reinstalling in a few weeks than I learned from years of computing. During the hours my system was out of commission, I was forced to such low-tech, high-touch activities as calling clients, completing a volunteer project, and reconnecting with friends. This resulted in more business, rekindled relationships, and much goodwill. Resorting to more pretechnological behavior, I often grabbed my yellow pad for a trip to the local coffeehouse. There I would write for hours with a freedom rarely available in my distracting office. (I even wrote a letter; remember letters?)

Yes, chaos brought me out of my comfort zone, out into the world, and into the twenty-first century—all with minimal injuries and tears. Not a bad ROI (return on investment), huh? Listen to the feedback and you will be so excited that you can't wait to roll up your sleeves and get your hands dirty.

Get Your Hands Dirty

The joy of gardening requires us to get down on our hands and knees and get our fingers in the soil. *Embrace Chaos* is an active principle. It is about throwing our arms wide open to life's bear hug, even if it's a hot, sticky hug, or one that momentarily knocks the breath out of us. Creativity and life do not happen from the sidelines. They happen in and all around us. In order to facilitate the growth of any collaborative creative process, including that of our own lives, we must participate to the fullest extent possible—get dirt under our fingernails and sweat on our brows.

And there's nothing like participation at work to send a clear message that you believe in the values you espouse, and are not too good to join your troupes in the creation trenches. It is not unusual for me to be called in by an executive or VP who recognizes an urgent need to help their teams and departments improve creativity and collaboration. It is unusual for that very executive or VP to show up for the "high priority" session. A last-minute phone call, meeting, or business trip pulls them away. In these cases I often hear grumbles that "the person who needs this most isn't here." The absent executive missed not only the content, but also the process so crucial to community and culture-building.

Find the Strange Attractor

Chaos feeds on participation—complete, sloppy, enthusiastic, sincere, unapologetic participation. The next chance you get, roll up those sleeves and dig in, and if you are paying attention you will even find the strange attractor. The order in chaos is sometimes only apparent when we have the larger view in mind. Nature gives us patterns represented as strange attractors. Your vision will yield such elegance if you allow it to unfold on its own terms. As a child I learned about the power of vision to organize a chaotic creative process. My father was an architect, and as he began designing a new home for the family, he wanted input from each of us. One Saturday at the breakfast table he said, "Tell me, Pamela, what do you want your room to look like?"

"What do you mean?," I questioned.

"Well, so far, we know that the house is going to have very high ceilings, and that one side will be completely glass so we can look out over the pond. The vision is to invite nature in."

"Hmmmmmm." I was at the height of my tomboyhood, and my eyes widened with the possibilities. "Well then, I don't want my room to have any walls."

"Interesting. How's that going to work?" he encouraged.

"Easy," I responded, "My room will be a platform hanging from the ceiling and the only way you will be able to get to it is by climbing a rope ladder."

My father, bless his heart, didn't say, "Now, honey, that's not very practical," or, "Think about the resale value." No, he happily (or diplomatically) went off to draft a plan for the house, which included my room hanging from the ceiling. In the weeks that followed, I remember more hours of talking and dreaming about the new house and what our lives would look like in it. I don't remember my father ever sitting me down and breaking the news that we would have to lose my hanging room. And in the end, I had a room with four walls and a door just like everyone else.

My father trusted that our shared vision would lead us all to the same place. He didn't see my crazy idea as a threat, or feel compelled to shut me down. Rather, the planning became an enormous opportunity for us all to participate in the evolution of the home we would share, and for the whole family to have a sense of ownership.

Participation, "team building," new learning, creative breakthroughs, and ownership are only a few of the many benefits you'll enjoy when you embrace chaos. Let your strange attractor, your vision, lead you to these fruits. With such wisdom, you, your coworkers, team members, staff, and entire organization will have the room to discover and respond to the challenges and opportunities hurtling your way this very moment.

---

1. Percival. "Chaos: A Science for the Real World." In *Exploring Chaos*, 12.
2. Vivaldi. "An Experiment with Mathematics." In *Exploring Chaos*, 33.

3. May. "The Chaotic Rhythms of Life." In *Exploring Chaos*, 94–95.
4. Lovins, Amory. "Fast Company Magazine." September, 1998, 88.
5. Wheatley and Kellner-Rogers, *A Simpler Way*, 13.
6. Robinson and Stern, 34–38.

For more than fifteen years, Jeff Hawkins, the visionary who gave birth to the PalmPilot, pursued his fascination. Rather than immediately beginning to design a handheld computer based on current assumptions in technology, he first studied a much more powerful and complex information system—the human brain. Applying insights pertaining to memory and under-standing, Hawkins developed a prototype that would spawn a huge new product line, one many thought impossible. Though he had several "Aha's!" along the way, clearly this was not an overnight success story. Failure, financial calamity, and frustration dotted the way. Hawkins stayed with his vision for fifteen years before it began to bare sustaining fruit. His thoughts on the journey? "Has it been worth it? As long as I am progressing toward my goals, doing good work, and having fun, then it's worth it. I have no regrets."[1]

SHOW UP AND PAY ATTENTION

*Be Here Now and Now and
Now and . . .*

| **THE PRINCIPLE** | This principle is not the grade school admonishment it might seem at first to be. Rather, it is an invitation to presence and to the presents of the present. Improviser Kelly Milani clarifies: "You don't live *for* the moment, but you live *in* the moment." *For* the moment assumes a payoff; *in* the moment is the payoff.

Show Up

Show Up and Pay Attention invites you to show up over time and in the moment. Hawkins does both. Showing up over time requires patience because, as Rilke counseled the young poet, "There is no meaning with time, no year matters, and ten years are nothing."[2]

When we show up over time, we live in the process, not the product. We do not search for the short-term solution or quick-fix success. We show up to our lives in the only way we can live them—one day at a time. We show up to our passion and allow it to move us. In time, and often before we expect it, our vision clears and the next step or task reveals itself. We gain access to the wisdom born of being.

When we do the process, the product does itself. In 1930 explorer Richard Byrd thanked his enthusiastic young student, Norman Vaughan, by naming a mountain peak after him. Sixty-five years after Vaughan promised himself he would someday climb his namesake mountain, he fulfilled his dream—at the age of 88. After the successful expedition, Vaughan told the press, "I want people to dream big, and I want them to dare to fail." He never abandoned his dream; he paid attention to find the right time to take action. Showing up is not a quick fix—it requires patience, vision, and presence.

Is all of this talk about the process trying your business soul? It certainly would try mine, unless I understood that valuing such intangibles does not exclude speed and innovation. Release yourself from limiting either-or preconceptions. Now, more than ever, your success depends on agility, flexibility, and rapid responsibility.

Show Up and Pay Attention is necessarily inclusive of these abilities. Your mind may need to stretch a bit to make room for the seemingly contradictory qualities of patience and speed, just as early physicists had to make room to understand the particle-wave phenomenon and to reconsider the nature of time as a variant in relativity theory. And, just as physicists allow for uncertainty and possibility of the particle in any given point in time, you will only find business and personal possibility when you arrive in this moment. Right here. Now.

Pay Attention

Presence is not simply physical; it demands our complete being, which leads to the second part of this principle: pay attention. When we become overly goal-oriented, we rarely give value to the present moment—to simply being. At times we forget altogether that we are human *beings*, not human *doings*.

To pay attention means to show up in the moment. Zen calls this "mindfulness," which is often described as "chopping wood and carrying water." When we carry water, we are present to just that— carrying water. When we chop wood, we are present to chopping wood. This singular availability opens the door for inspiration.

Would Jeff Hawkins be celebrating the introduction of the fifth PalmPilot model (as of this writing) if he had not shown up? Would you have been able to order this book or other goods and services on-line had Jeff Bezos, amazon.com's founder, and other E-commerce pioneers not paid attention? Have you or your business missed any opportunities because you were not home when the opportunity knocked? Would you know? Unfortunately, inspiration doesn't leave a sticky note on your door, as does my UPS driver, to notify you the idea you ordered has arrived.

Creativity won't be delivered if you are not present for it. If the inspiration tree falls in the forest and you aren't there to hear it, it falls in silence. In the observer-created universe, opportunities don't exist when you are not there to bare witness. Like at many charity raffles, you must be present to win; your attention is required.

You will *not* notice creative possibility without showing up— whether you are thinking about your quarterly report when your customer is relaying a problem, or responding to E-mail when your employee is sharing a news flash from the front lines. Sure, you'll clear off your desk by the end of the day and no one will be home to accept the delivery. You must show up for creativity if it is to exist at all. Listen to writer Anne Lamott's call to attention:

> There is ecstasy in paying attention. . . . Anyone who wants to can be surprised by the beauty or pain of the natural world, of the human mind and heart, and can try to capture just that— the details, the nuance, what is. If you look around, you will start to see.[3]

Anyone who wants to? Sign me up!

Some years ago my Essence beckoned me with these very words: "Pay attention," it broadcasted, "Look up, look around you!" It called me to notice coincidence and pay attention to opportunities, to feelings and experiences, and to the response of close friends as I shared an evolving vision to take my work in improvisational theater to a new audience. I heard increasing urgency in this message to pay attention. I knew that soon it would take more energy not to listen, than to follow its call. Wisely, I gave in with little fight and began a journey in learning and teaching that continues to this day.

At times the information was rather mundane. Other times it helped me through major blocks, such as the time I was struggling to find the opening for an article. I took a break from my work and went to the gym. When I arrived, I stretched a bit, then walked up to the stair-climber, ready to start my workout. The digital message scrolled across the electronic panel read, "Just step right up and start climbing!" "That's it!" I said to myself. "That is exactly what I need to do with my article!" Instead of pondering and trying to come up with the perfect opening, I needed to "step right up and start writing." I'm not suggesting a cosmic order programmed just the right message for me, the center of the universe. I am suggesting that when we do show up and pay attention, we can take advantage of almost any information and allow it to propel us beyond our sometimes tedious self-referential stagnation.

Collective Presence

We can also experience the power of attention in group or community settings where the collective presence allows us to tap into much more than we alone can access. Whether cocreating a work of art or working individually in the presence of others, focused group attention has great power. Beginning creative writing students are often amazed at the reservoir of experiences available to them when they write in a group. "I didn't think I had anything to say, but when I started moving my pen across the page, the words just kept coming!" reported one recent group-writing convert.

We also feel the power of collective presence in peer support groups. Feelings and insights inaccessible when a person is alone often emerge with the safety and attention of the group. Likewise, many meditation practitioners report more powerful experiences meditating with a group than on their own. When an entire group shows up, the power of attention multiplies exponentially.

The birth impulse of team-based work cultures was the recognition that collaboration and group focus on challenges often revealed possibilities and innovations that rarely showed themselves to individuals. Unfortunately, today many of these same well-intentioned groups dilute their power either through judgment and internal conflict, or rigid agendas that leave little room for discovery.

Nonlocal Causality

Quantum physicists have discovered phenomena that by analogy further illuminate the power of attention and its role in creativity in an interconnected universe. Here's how attention manifests in physics: It is known that the polarization or spin of a subatomic particle may fluctuate randomly between two possible directions. At the same time, some atomic processes produce two particles whose spins are oppositely directed. Quantum theory predicts that when one such particle reverses its spin, so does the other at exactly the same time. Experiments on protons and polarized light confirm that the two particles always have opposite spin or polarization, even if they become widely separated. Somehow the particles remain associated although they are not together spatially. Whatever reverses the spin of one particle at one location simultaneously reverses the spin of the other particle at the other location.[4] In other words, the particles actually pay attention to each other over infinite time and distance.

It does not matter whether the two particles in question are across the atom or across the universe from one another. The spin of one will always be opposite to the spin of the other. Neither does it appear to matter when these particles were once joined. Particles produced during the big bang may now be in atoms of separate objects, people, or even planets, but they still maintain opposite spins. Thus is born the concept of "nonlocal causality." Unlike the mechanistic version of cause and effect, this causal influence appears to act instantaneously. This defies Einstein's theory of relativity, which predicts that no signal can travel instantaneously (or specifically, faster than the speed of light).[5] The ultimate extension of this phenomenon is that everything and everyone in the universe is interconnected and unfathomable!

Drawing an analogy from the quantum model, it may also be true that our inspirations are equally untraceable. Just as the same unknowable cause affects the spin of a particle here and on the other side of the country, we cannot always track the cause of the idea or inspiration that comes to us in the shower or while we daydream at the beach. However, when we pay attention, these thoughts and images become the fuel for our creativity.

Formative Causation

It becomes even more interesting: in the early 1980s Rupert Sheldrake began to explore nonlocal causality using his hypothesis of "formative causation." He discovered such mysteries as rats who were taught a new trick in one place apparently made it easier for rats elsewhere to learn the same trick. Similarly, chemical solutions that crystallized for the first time in one location appeared to make it easier for subsequent crystallization in another location, regardless of the distance between the initial crystallizing solution and later ones. In addition to these and other verifiable examples, history has recorded many cases of discoveries made simultaneously in different parts of the world. How far can this be from the experience of individuals and groups who regularly come to the same "Aha!" at once?

Creative impulses and inspiration appear to travel across great distances (be they physical, cultural, spiritual, or otherwise) without impediment. And, like the polarized particle, the information we need to determine our own creative spin is available at any given moment, if we simply make ourselves available to it as we show up and pay attention.

Just as subatomic particles are interconnected, so, too, are we as members of our communities—global, local, familial, educational, commercial, and creative, to name only a few. In any living system the individual and collaborative creative process demands participation, awareness, attention, and availability. Organic living systems are open systems that must constantly exchange matter and energy with other systems in order to grow. The same is true with the living creative process. We must show up to it and participate in it for it to evolve and surprise us. If we do not pay attention, the sometimes subtle, sometimes glaringly obvious, messages of the universe will evade us. Paying attention will not be easy if we are living under the influence of learned blocks.

| LEARNED BLOCKS |

Just Do It!

Just Do It! No, you didn't accidentally skip ahead to the Doing Things Differently section of this chapter. While this Madison Avenue slogan is great for motivating (and selling sneakers), it can also send us leaping over opportunity or forging ahead just for the forging, when we really need to just *not* do it or anything else for that matter. Whether your "not doing" is a temporary response to the after-lunch slump or an intuitive resistance to move ahead on a project, it is worthy of attention.

If you are stalled, it is often for good reason. Pay attention to the information. Are you tired? Rest. Are you crabby? Take a break. Has your creative bloom begun to wilt? Give it some water and air. The press releases from your creative collaboration can come in many different forms; learn to notice them. Rather than plodding on, listen. The time you take away, the time you spend stopping, will be made up manyfold when you return.

As a writer, I can tell you that the difference between one morning and the next at the keyboard can be the difference between a nose dive into despair and euphoric flow. By paying attention, I can discern between a particularly difficult segment that I simply need to continue to show up to, and an idea that is not moving, because it is simply not the time. While I continue to discourage prescriptive responses to creativity, I encourage you to show up and pay attention to the many time- and angst-saving suggestions broadcast from the process itself. Simple—not easy. Especially if you have learned isolation.

Isolation

Withdrawing into your office, or away from community, friends, and family, is a surefire way to avoid intimacy—not only with others, but with yourself and in turn, with your creativity. Withdrawing in response to a challenge or for quiet reflection is useful for a time. It is a block when isolation becomes your drug of choice, removing you from the support and life-giving input available to you.

The very people we remove ourselves from are the ones most able to reflect reality and restore hope when necessary. Unfortunately, such avoidance cuts us off not only from valuable information we need to move through our challenges, but also from the love and support that only those who know us well can offer.

Some withdraw abruptly, leaving friends to ask, "Hey, has anyone heard from so-and-so lately?" Others isolate by omission, not building a network in the first place. With largely work-related acquaintances, they don't socialize outside of the office or participate in other activities where intimate friendships might develop. Or perhaps a recent move has left them without a familiar support network. Or perhaps the isolation is subtler still.

I've been there. In high school I became a master self-isolator, while masquerading as a healthy, active teenager. My parents were going through a bitter and prolonged separation, followed by a bitter and prolonged divorce. I saw the world that I had always known and taken for granted crumble around me. Though I had wonderful friends, I felt I could not risk letting them in on my misery. I chose to shut the door on my feelings, rather than risk losing control.

It took me years to dismantle the fortress I built to protect myself from those feelings. I began with baby steps, risking telling my story to a close friend or partner and eventually sharing more of myself to a growing community of others who were also remembering their lives. I discovered that participating in community means risk and responsibility. I also discovered that without community, I survive; as a member of a community, I *live*.

Isolation is not only a threat to your personal, emotional health, but a barrier to the health of your work life, as well. (Didn't I say I wasn't going to let you off the hook by separating your work life from the rest of your wonderful being?) Isolation at work cuts you off from the pulse of the organization. Despite rumors to the contrary, every organization has one. Even if it is faint, it can support your own creative heartbeat and rekindle your passion. In isolation you will never benefit from its sustaining rhythm and flow.

Regardless of how and why isolation occurs, the outcome is the same: we stew in our own self-referential juices. Perhaps this gives us the illusion that we have it all under control. Besides, we don't want to burden anyone else with our troubles. This approach may work for a while. Soon, however, after our only input comes from distorted perceptions, we spiral into a negative view of ourselves, work, and life itself. This worldview becomes a self-fulfilling prophecy. Like a bad neighborhood, you shouldn't go to this place alone.

Quantum physicists discovered that when they try to isolate subatomic parts they no longer behave as they naturally would as part of the subatomic whole. In the same way, our thoughts and behavior can become distorted when we isolate ourselves and stop participating in community. Here we remember that we are, after all, human—that others have had similar feelings and experiences. We cannot learn these lessons in isolation.

Community is participatory; it demands that we show up and pay attention. Just as the creative process thrives on participation, so, too, does the life of any community. What a wonderful place for us to practice intimacy with and *response*ability to ourselves and to our fellow players.

Truck Driving

You may not be isolating, but you may as well be if you learned truck driving. A sure indicator of whether or not you are in your body—in the here and now—is the number of bruises and scrapes on your extremities. When you do not show up and pay attention, you bump into tables, chairs, doorways, you name it; if it's in your path, you'll run into it, break it, spill it, step on it, or lose it! When we are not showing up, we drive our bodies like they are big rusty, dented-up, dump trucks. We are careless, unworried about scratching the finish—what's one more dent? No one will notice. We back into the garbage cans and shrubbery of life without any concern for consequences.

Of course, there are consequences. We are getting *through* life, rather than showing up for it. Like the time last year when I set out to walk the dog with the intention of dropping off my dry cleaning and mailing some bills in the box outside the cleaners. My presence was anywhere but in the present as I plowed into my day—a fact I discovered when I "came to" just before completely stuffing my dry cleaning into the mail box! I still smile as I contemplate my explanation to the postal carrier.

What's your version of truck driving? Do you put your eighteen wheeler in gear when you arrive at your workplace? Do you make a list and begin rolling through it, or perhaps head off in whatever direction the first round of E-mails, morning meetings, and phone messages send you? Are you behind the wheel, but not really aware of where you are or where you're going? While there may be hundreds of things beyond your control in any given day calling you to respond quickly and to chuck your neatly scribed to-do list, you can still go along for the ride.

Mood Altering Substances

With similar results to truckdriving, some of us learned mood altering substances can aid creativity. If this block doesn't belong to you and certainly isn't an issue in your work, you may be tempted to skip this section. I hope you'll read on anyway; the tentacles of this impediment reach farther than you may know.

A creative life is an intimate life. It requires you to be available to yourself on a level that many would just as soon avoid. I believe that the romance surrounding the tortured, starving, and drug-addicted artist has evolved in response to the fear of this intimacy. There are too many tales of artists who met their demise through addiction, to support the idea that drug-induced states facilitate creativity beyond the superficial. It is not just the drugs that block creativity, but the belief system that grows up around this life-threatening disease. See if you recognize yourself in any of these reflections of recovering addicts:

Part of the progression of the disease was that I didn't do what I loved. [My addiction] cut me off from people and my self-esteem—from my own gifts. Before recovery, I had some creative opportunities at work, but I didn't know what I liked, so I ignored it. I was dying. It was a creative/spiritual death.

—Mara, lawyer and artist

I was constantly focused outside of myself. I felt I was responsible for making everyone else happy. It started when I was a child with my mom, and that just continued. I was always focused on "How do I look?" and that translated into "How do I feel?" They had to tell me how I felt. I tried harder and harder to manipulate the outcome. It was exhausting.

—Cindy, communication adviser

I always thought that being a starving artist was part of the dues you had to pay. I don't think that anymore. It wasn't helpful to my creativity. What's different today is not so much that the ideas are more fluid or that there are more of them. What's different is I'm able to get them done, to trust my instincts—not water down or second-guess my ideas.

—Michael, furniture designer

Addicts do not have a corner on the blocked creativity market. If you have ever cut yourself off from your intuition or acted in someone else's best interest rather than your own, you have a share in this market.

Each of the people I interviewed described the road back to their inner joy and creativity as a spiritual recovery process; a process of peeling away the layers that kept them from fully participating in their lives. Day by day, step by step, they were each able to show up and pay attention to the riches of the moment.

Avoidance and Procrastination

As harmless as it seemed, we may also have danced with avoidance and procrastination. My friend, Toba, is fond of the familiar saying, When the going gets tough, the tough go shopping. She's onto something. There are many ways we can avoid showing up and paying attention, besides the use of numbing substances. We use other processes to distract ourselves from what Ann Wilson Schaef calls, "knowing what we know and feeling what we feel." Busyness, debting and spending, sex, food, exercise, work, and other people can all be effective tools of avoidance. Whatever our drug of choice, the outcome is the same: we are cut off from our Essence, the subtle (and not-so-subtle) voices that lead us from within and without. Cindy expands on her experience of this block:

> I was addicted to my relationship. Everything depended on how that was going. Growing up in the fifties you were trained for that. You had to get picked. You could consider jobs as a nurse, teacher, or librarian, but you didn't think about a career. You were trained that you were going to be a wife and mother. It started out with school dances. You weren't OK if you didn't get picked. You had to strive for your external person. What was going on inside didn't matter.

Avoidance takes us away from our Essence, away from our dreams. Procrastination is an equally painful form of avoidance for many, with an extra helping of self-loathing and guilt: "I really *should* start that sales report," "I don't know why I can't make myself get into my art studio lately," "I *must* organize the piles on my desk." We procrastinate about things we love to do just as much as about those we don't. This obsessive energy is the flipside of work addiction; it paralyzes us. The impact, however, is the same as it is on the compulsive worker; it cuts us off from a deeper experience of our joy. We begin to define ourselves by what we are (or are not) doing and judge ourselves accordingly.

Again, relief begins by simply doing things differently.

| DOING THINGS DIFFERENTLY |

Be Transformable

In my work as an educator and writer, I offer my students, clients, audiences, and readers opportunities to transform in response to my message. I hope they will be available to make new connections and discoveries and find their way to positive change if they are in need of it.

Though I, and many other messengers, encourage transformation in others, we don't always hold ourselves to the same standard of transform-ability. Your work is probably more similar to mine than you know. Each of your collaborations, each of your leadership opportunities, offers you the chance to be both the facilitator of transformation, and the transformed. In fact, I do not think you can be an effective leader or collaborator if your transformation door doesn't swing both ways. In other words, to transform the way you work, you must be willing to be transformed by your work.

During flights back from speaking or consulting engagements, I take time to reflect on the experience. A few years ago I found myself unsettled. The client was thrilled with the results, the audience evaluations were very positive, and I had met or exceeded all expectations and objectives. But it didn't quite sit with me. Something was missing. What was it? Had I not prepared enough? Had I not delivered some pivotal insight? Had I tried to accomplish too much in the available time? What . . . ahha! It dawned on me—*I* was missing. Though everything looked and sounded great from the outside, I was not completely present, available, and transformable on the inside. Perhaps I was too attached to my agenda or fearful of losing control of the outcomes. For whatever reason, on some subtle level, I was not available to be transformed along with the group. I was not a partner in learning, in cocreating the experience along with my fellow collaborators. The humbling discovery deepened my commitment to practice what I teach. Simple—not easy.

Be Unimportant

Though your work may not regularly put you in front of audiences, you also have a transformation door that can remain well-oiled if you show up and pay attention. You will continue to grow as you inspire others' creative contributions and allow yourself to receive the gifts that come through your door on the return swing. To receive these gifts, you yourself may need to check something at the door. You may need to be unimportant.

Self-importance, self-centeredness, and that darn ego will cut you off from presence as quickly as any other block. You want to show up, not show off. A lesson from improvisation supports me in being in the moment when I work. Improvisers know they cannot succeed if they try to shine as individuals. They must show up with the singular intention of making everyone else look good. Guided by service, improvisers can take advantage of the possibilities within each heightened stage moment without self-consciousness or agenda. For just this reason, I sometimes place a gentle reminder on a sticky note within eyeshot during a presentation, "It's not about you."

It's not about you, either. While you are responsible to your creative collaborations, you are not responsible *for* them. Yes, you help define the vision and maybe even approve the final action plan. You are not, however, in charge of how the collaboration unfolds, who has what inspiration, or how each individual experiences him- or herself along the way. You can cocreate a safe environment; you cannot orchestrate all that happens within it, lest you want to stifle the very possibilities you set out to explore.

So be unimportant. Know yourself in relation to a larger context. Gain perspective. Be a grain of sand on a vast beach on a large planet in a gigantic solar system within an infinite universe. How important do you feel now? Notice how the space all around you expands? It's no coincidence. The room you have for creativity is directly proportional to the level of unimportance you allow yourself.

Be Patient

In this expansive place, doing things differently may not be about *doing* anything. So be patient. Showing up is a process. In twelve-step circles, early recovery is sometimes described as "I came. I came to. I came to believe [in a power greater than myself]." First we need to simply show up physically. Slowly the fog of learned blocks lifts and a greater wisdom emerges, one that guides where our vision once failed.

The wisdom you need for your work and life success will be revealed on just the right schedule. Though sometimes difficult to accept, this is creativity's version of information delivered on a need-to-know basis. I am not talking about the information overload available to you twenty-four hours a day, but the most useful knowledge only available when you pay attention. When you think nothing is happening, often it is only that there is nothing you can see, or that the process is moving so slowly, it appears to be not moving at all. If we do not get immediate gratification, we sometimes give up before the movement is apparent. We don't stick with our new healthy eating plan, we stop our exercise program, we don't finish the dissertation—it's taking too long, where's the progress, it's too hard, what's the point, anyway?

We forget that the creative process happens one moment at a time. And the showing up is cumulative, sometimes quite tangibly and other times not. Though I often have only a few hours each day to write, by the end of the week I have several written pages—pages I would not have written at all had I not had the patience to show up day after day.

Notice

One way to show up in the moment is to notice. You can teach yourself to pay attention. The first night of class, I ask my beginning improvisation students to take a few minutes to concentrate on each of their senses. One by one we work through them—first listening for all of the sounds—the plane passing overhead, footsteps in the hallway, one classmate's breathing, another's rustling clothes, a pencil rolling off a desk. Then we move to our sense of touch—the temperature in the room, the clothes on our body, our jewelry, our teeth, our hair.

When we concentrate each individual sense, we clear out the cobwebs and reinvigorate each sense. We may be amazed at how many details we were missing. At work, or in any familiar surrounding, challenge yourself to notice three new things about your surroundings. You'll be surprised how much you never really saw before. We have all of the resources we need to gather information—we just have to remember to use them! For some, this becomes an invitation to meditate.

Meditate

Daily meditation is a powerful way to practice showing up and paying attention. Set aside time each day simply to *be*. Soon you will find the peacefulness of meditation seeping into other areas of your life.

There are many ways to meditate, formal and informal. Whether you embark on a lifelong practice of Zen meditation or simply take quiet time each day, the most important thing is that you do it. Take time to *Listen to Your Essence,* for without this deep connection, you overlook the most important impulses of your creative process. Many workplaces today are supporting meditation and quiet reflection. Check and see if the opportunity exists, or create one.

Many forms of meditation begin and end with a heightened awareness of the breath. Breathing leads us back to our center—to feeling, insight, and beyond to a place transcending all thought and feeling. With practice, we can quickly reconnect to our Essence by gently returning our attention to our breath.

William Hanrahan reminds us:

> *When we start focusing on our breathing, we interrupt the mental process and the emotional process—we change the physical process. That's why breathing has always been taught as the first step to meditation, because it calms the mind, the body, and the emotions . . . It allows us not only to observe ourselves more accurately, but to observe our surroundings. It deepens our listening, both internally and externally.*

When we pay attention to something we do unconsciously, we raise our level of self-awareness. We have choices again; we are restored to freedom and an awareness of all possibilities.

Go to the Salon—Creative Community

If meditation restores us to sanity, fellowship can restore us to humanity. Maybe it's time to go to the salon. I'm not suggesting a new hairdo (though it may be time for that, too). I'm talking about forming your own community for conscious creativity. The fabled salons of the mid- and late nineteenth century provided aristocratic women a forum to meet, exchange ideas, and showcase their creativity in an era when few other opportunities existed for them. Paris in the twenties and thirties brought together Gertrude Stein,

Hemingway, Picasso, and many others for endless café meetings and Saturday afternoon soirees. At the same time, the renowned Algonquin Hotel's round table convened with the likes of Dorothy Parker, Lillian Hellman, George Kaufman, and Moss Hart. Throughout the ages, people have come together in community to foster and bare witness to creative work, and to support those who dared to press beyond society's expectations.

You, too, can plumb the depths of creative community. Join in! Even soloists need feedback and collaborative energy. Be purposeful or casual. You may choose to institutionalize a creative resource center, as the IdeaVerse founders did, or allow lunchtime conversations to evolve for mutual support and cheerleading.

Inspired by the work of Natalie Goldberg, my friend Paul has formed a "Freewriting" group. He meets with like-minded friends and coworkers and brings along a stack of books. One of the group members opens a book and randomly points to a sentence. For the next five to thirty minutes everyone writes a story (or whatever comes to mind) using that sentence as their opening line. Often the writing is raw and unformed. It is never meant to be anything but that. The point is to harness the power of the group for creative focus. Often, seeds for compelling new work, beginnings demanding more time and attention, and long-sealed doors cracked open to invite exploration, lie within the handwritten pages.

Some workplace groups now provide similar safe-havens. Coworkers meet to share ideas-in-progress in an arena where trust and nonjudgment are hallmarks. One fall a group of my friends and I started an informal "Visions Group." We met regularly at a neighborhood coffee shop to share our lives-in-progress, discuss our dreams, and commit to action steps for their attainment. The early drafts of this book were nurtured there. We all need a cheerleader or two. Why not form your own personal cheerleading squad?

Ask a new (or old) friend out for coffee, for a walk, or for a bike ride. Put up a sign at work to find a tennis, golf, or fishing partner.

Join a bowling league or go play bingo. Volunteer to clean up your neighborhood (or someone else's), tutor in an after-school program, or work on a political campaign. Or just take a little more time to get to know your neighbors: stop for a chat when you shovel snow or walk the dog. Take time to visit with a neighbor who is having a slow period during his sidewalk sale or who is planting a garden.

Community is built over time and by showing up. It matters not what your community looks like; what's important is that it's there. The power is in the collective presence. Once again, no one can do it alone. And even if we could do it alone, why would we want to?

Embrace Mystery

In community you may also find the courage to embrace mystery. A colleague at DePaul University recently had an opportunity to do just this. In the midst of a hectic quarter of teaching, research, and committee obligations, Marisa took a three-day retreat at a convent on the campus of St. Mary's in South Bend, Indiana. The campus was all but deserted; the academic year had just ended and the retreat house had few guests. The only contact she had was with an occasional elderly nun who lived and worked at the retreat house.

Marisa got just the break she needed—lots of solitude and time for long walks and reflection. She found two big trees on the edge of a field next to a small stream. Always prepared for such opportunities, Marisa strung the hammock she kept in her car between the spreading trunk of a huge old oak tree and spent one morning writing in her journal and enjoying the quiet. As noon approached, she tucked her journal in her backpack and wound her hammock around it. She knew it would be safe. After all, she hadn't seen a single soul all day and she was in a fairly remote area.

Marisa walked back to the retreat house and ate in silence with the sisters. After lunch she returned to her secluded spot to find that her hammock had not been disturbed. She settled in, pulled out her journal, and reread her thoughts from the morning. At the end of her last passage, her jaw dropped. Written with her own pen by another hand were the words, "You are headed in the correct direction. Continue on." Signed, "God."

Her mind began to fly through the possibilities. "Who went through my things? What a violation! How dare they? Did one of the elderly nuns tromp all the way out here just to give me this message? Who do they think they are? Or could it be that God actually took the time to communicate directly with me?" It was a waste of time to try to solve the mystery, she realized. What a distraction! She smiled to herself and to whom or whatever visited her, closed her journal, and chose to embrace the mystery and wonder of the event and to pay attention to the message.

Our messages may not always be delivered directly or be signed "God." And when we pay attention, we see messages everywhere. All we need to do is show up—to *be*.

---

1. Hawkins, 108.
2. Rilke, 30.
3. Lamott, 100-101.
4. Gribbin, 229.
5. Capra, 323.

**I have dinner with a friend at a Japanese restaurant.** After we wash our hands with the traditional steaming _oshi bori_, I notice the woman and her two young children at the table next to us. One of the little girls plays with her white cloth, first rolling it, then folding it, then draping it over her arm, as if she is a wine server in an expensive restaurant. It then became an ice rink for imaginary skaters and, later, a veil to hide behind. Throughout the rest of my meal, I glance over at the other table and smile, as the little girl explores every dimension and possibility of the washcloth for over an hour.

MAKE CONTINUOUS DISCOVERIES

Cultivate Curiosity

| **THE PRINCIPLE** | We don't need to be taught how to be creative. Possibilities unfold before us from the first moment we engage with our environment. The little girl was not *trying* to be creative, and she certainly was not *trying* to play. She was, of course, not trying to do anything; she was exploring, making discoveries, and enjoying herself.

Wonder

Ever wonder why the memory of the first date stays with you for years in all of its detail, as does the first visit to a new city or restaurant, or first day at a new school or job? We *expect* the unknown in new experiences; we have our radars finely tuned for as many revelations as possible. Once the new is familiar, we stop vigilantly checking the radar screen. We no longer expect to be surprised. And guess what? We aren't!

After a short time at work, you, too, may find the newness of your challenges and responsibilities wearing off. Just as your job begins to lose its "new car smell," you settle into the routine. You've gotten used to the new dashboard, adjusted the seat to your liking, tuned the radio to your station—the sparkle is gone, and now its just another vehicle to "get you there." Unfortunately, there is no "there" there without discovery on the way. *Continuous* discovery.

Continuous discovery is wonder. In 1995 the story of the "milk miracle" spread throughout India. A woman went to her temple with a customary offering of milk for one of the Hindu statues. She held the milk up to the statue's mouth and witnessed it drinking. The milk actually disappeared into the statue's mouth. Within hours the news spread throughout the country. Office buildings closed, and thousands of people flocked to their temples. Many others witnessed the same phenomenon. The next day Indian newspapers trumpeted headlines of the "milk miracle."

It is not important whether or not the statues actually drank the milk (as with all mysterious phenomena, experts immediately came forth with their attempts to explain away the occurrence). It *is* important that an entire country enjoyed and celebrated the possibility of a miracle and with it restored themselves to lively relationships with their lives and work.

In the struggle to enliven creativity at work, it is no surprise that most people have to reach back to childhood to remember experiences of wonder. We don't have much use for wonder in adulthood; this is our loss. A student shared the memory of when she, her brother, and cousins had decided that every Sunday afternoon between one and five o'clock would be "the magic hours." During that time anything was possible. She recounts:

It was during this time that we realized odd things would occur; a certain atmosphere would settle upon us and things out of the ordinary would happen. Now that I look back, it was just that we became aware of our creative process and responded to it. But it really did seem like magic.

The awareness of the *possibility* of magic and an attitude of wonder transforms what we may otherwise experience as ordinary into the extraordinary. Here, the truly original is dis-covered.

Nobel Prize–winning physician Albert Szent-Györgyi defines discovery as "Looking at the same thing as everyone else and seeing something different." Discovery enabled Newton to perceive gravity upon seeing an apple fall from a tree. Discovery inspired Einstein to consider time as a variable in the theory of relativity. Discovery led Max Planck to experiment with light, setting the stage for the quantum revolution in physics. None of these people were the first to witness the phenomenon that triggered their inspiration. They *were* the first to witness it with an active attitude of wonder and a willingness to make new discoveries. Had any of them, or countless other pioneers, expected to see what they had already seen or to learn what they already knew, we would not enjoy the fruits of their discoveries today.

The little girl with the washcloth, the devout Hindus, the children at play, and the quantum physicists all practiced the principle of *Make Continuous Discoveries*. They teach us that we can choose to create environments of wonder and discovery just as easily as we create environments of predictability, cynicism, and judgment.

Positive Environments

Throughout this book stories describe the characteristics of positive environments for creativity and collaboration. In addition to being a dynamic network of people who support and practice the principles of creativity, such an environment must be a place that fosters a lively awareness of possibilities. It must be a place of discovery.

Anesthesia technician by day and improviser by night, Kelly Milani looks for the same qualities of respect, trust, and collaboration in the operating room as she does on stage:

> *I want some other forms of mental stimulation and interactive fun when I'm at work. I don't mean shooting rubber bands at the doctors or compromising the decorum of my very serious work environment, but I need to be able to have fun and "play" with my coworkers. . . . I think things flow a lot more smoothly when people are able to laugh with one another and be together on the common ground of humor. I find that not only does it help me deal with stress, it actually helps me to communicate. For example, you can't have a nurse who is cowering, who is afraid to interact with a surgeon because of their difference in status. That throws off the whole performance of the operating room—the efficiency of it.*

You may not want your surgeon improvising with your operation, or your accountant improvising with your tax return; you *do*, however, want to put your trust in skilled professionals who can think on their feet and respond quickly to new or unexpected information. This is why *Make Continuous Discoveries* is the cornerstone of stage improvisation. Novice improvisers sometimes fear they won't be able to think of anything to say or do when they get in front of an audience. They soon learn that they don't need to make something happen or think of something brilliant—for one thing, there's just no time. Milani shares:

> *When someone else is out on stage and their scene starts to go bad and they get that look on their face like, "OK, help me here," you can't stop and try to think of something funny. You have to just step out there. You can't let them fall! You just step out there and help them. A lot of times I've done that and it can be scary;*

I don't know what the hell I'm going to say. I just step out and do it. You have to give your subconscious some credit.

Give yourself credit for your ability to *Make Continuous Discoveries* and to fuel the ever-evolving creative process. What a way to work! Do you trust your colleagues not to let you fall? To "just step right out there" and help you? Can *they* trust you to do the same? Without such trust, there is little room for discovery.

In robust economies, current and prospective employees look for workplaces that support creativity and provide resources for continuous discovery. While these qualities need to be woven into the fabric of the organization, they must also be reinforced through formal training programs. Training is not a panacea for a dismal environment, nor is it a luxury. Patty Frett, Anderson Consulting's director of recruiting agrees training is an important issue for recruiting, as well as for client service. "They [prospective hires] want to know if their company is going to ensure that their skills are state of the art." She adds, "Training is a constant for our people because you can't meet a client with last year's skill set. It devalues your product."[1]

In an age where long-term employer-employee loyalty is rare, continuous discovery takes on an even greater value. Eric Rolfe Greenberg, director of management studies for the American Management Association in New York, reports, "Successful companies recruit and retain employees not by guaranteeing employment but employability—the ongoing development of skills and competencies which becomes part of the employee's portable toolkit."[2]

You deserve a workplace that supports continuous discovery. You deserve to work with people who challenge you to see farther than you have seen before. You deserve mentors who set a high bar when it comes to discovery. In college, I had just such an opportunity. I worked as an assistant on Romanian director André Serban's production of *The Three Sisters* at the American Repertory Theatre in Cambridge, Massachusetts. There I learned an early lesson in the power (and threat) of *Make Continuous Discoveries*. Throughout rehearsal Serban experimented with new approaches to each scene, to each character, and to the play itself. This challenged the actors, designers, and production staff on a daily basis. Props, scenery, and costume pieces were discarded and new ones requested daily through to opening night. The actors rarely had an opportunity to run through a scene the same way twice. (Serban reasoned that there would be plenty of time for that once the show opened; rehearsal was a time for exploration!) Engaged in continuous discovery himself, Serban challenged each collaborator to do the same.

Recalling formative experiences in her career, Cherry Jones, who played Irena in that production, described it as

> *. . . one of those productions that is sort of a watershed for everyone . . . We were all quite young at the time, and it was just one of those remarkable experiences that we all look back on with a great deal of nostalgia. It keeps me from ever really wanting to do that play again, because I think we really arrived at that very difficult balance with Chekhov between comedy and tragedy.[3]*

More Than Improvement

Long-running shows stay alive by actors who *Make Continuous Discoveries*, who must find something new in a character, the story, and the relationships on stage each night to keep performances fresh. You think *you* get bored at work? What if you had to say the same words, make the same movements, and wear the same clothes eight times a week, hundreds of times each year, *and* make it appear each time as though you were doing it for the very first time?

You may have more in common with this challenge than you know. We all perform in some equivalent to the long-running show; work, family, and relationships will stagnate or flourish based on our willingness to be surprised. What if you thought of your work as a long-running show that you needed to keep fresh by making new discoveries and contributions each day? And what if there would be hundreds in line eager to relieve you of your duties if you didn't keep your work fresh? You have just as many opportunities in *your* life and work to make "first time" discoveries as does an actor (even if you don't get a round of applause at the end of your workday).

Make Continuous Discoveries has a counterpart in Total Quality Management, which is founded on the principle of continuous improvement. Continuous discovery includes improvements and takes it further. Yes, it's important to continuously look for opportunities to improve each process, product, and service. And, yes, it is insufficient to simply fix what is broken, congratulate yourself, then sit back and relax until it breaks again. You are familiar with the wisdom of improvement.

You may be less familiar with *discovery*. While improvement necessarily refers to an existing product or process (as does defining a problem), discovery enables a quantum leap to an entirely new possibility. The earlier noted discovery of aspartame's chemistry is one of hundreds of examples—no problem had been defined; no causal framework established beyond the happy conditions for an "Aha!" Just as subatomic particles simply cease to exist in one energy state, and reappear in another without passing through the space in between, discovery allows your inspiration to simply appear without referents of time, space, and preexisting conditions.

So as you limber up your discovery muscles, do not limit yourself to making discoveries about what you already know—what meanders past your field of vision or within earshot. That is only a start, a good one, but just a start. As you achieve greater flexibility, you will find yourself living in a state of discovery available to both linear and Quantum Creativity. Here, well tuned and toned from listening to your Essence, you can transcend the apparent limitations of what is, what has been done before, and what is believed possible. You can continuously discover what was previously obscured.

By now it is all too clear how *Make Continuous Discoveries* can transform the way you work. For some, however, it is difficult to practice, because of learned blocks.

| LEARNED BLOCKS |

Don't Ask Questions

Have you ever been told by a parent, teacher, or a colleague, "*Don't Ask Questions.*"! You are not alone if you have. Many of us had our innate questioning, curiosity, and mystery-seeking attitude *taught* out of us. Somewhere mixed in with "Sit up straight," "Wash your hands before dinner," and "Don't talk with your mouth full," was the implication that questions were impolite at best, and "out of the question" at worst. (Notice how that familiar phrase connotes *impossibility*? When was the last time you heard someone exclaim, "Now that's *in* the question!"?) We learned that it is more important to fit in and to give the right answer, than to live in the questions, follow our passion, and explore uncharted territories.

I hear from clients' employees that they routinely begin work projects with less than the needed information, because they are afraid to ask "dumb" questions. They would rather try to get the information on the sly or figure it out on their own, than appear not to know all the answers. With the assumption that the answers are more important than the questions, a climate of fear takes root. Misinformation, wasted time and resources, and frustrated workers (not to mention customers!) become the trademark here. One interior designer complained that the climate was so competitive in her new firm that she couldn't even get someone to show her how to use the blueprint machine! The culture sent a clear message that it was "every man for himself." More missed opportunities for discovery; more limited possibilities. I don't know about you, but I hope my bank teller, insurance representative, and health care providers aren't afraid to ask questions in the interest of delivering the best service.

Fear of Looking Stupid

Another reason some resist asking questions is a related learned block reaching epidemic proportions: fear of looking stupid. Where did this deep-seated fear start and why is it so debilitating? In early childhood we got the message that there was a "right" and a "wrong" way to behave if we wanted to fit in or receive positive attention.

By the time we encounter educational, religious, or other social institutions, we have a pretty good idea of what stupid looks like and an even stronger idea of not wanting to be caught dead looking that way. When we start our work lives, we are experts at surveying the organizational landscape and shaping ourselves to fit yet another set of expectations. By now the stakes may be even higher than before. In many organizational cultures, foolishness means loss of respect, credibility, or even loss of a job. Why would we risk appearing to know less than everything or asking dumb questions in such a climate?

With all the talk about innovation and risk-taking today, you'd think people would come out of the woodwork with their questions and ideas. They don't, won't, and can't, unless they face down this demon.

Dualistic Thinking

Perhaps you are paralyzed by dualistic thinking. When you see only two options, you may be stuck in a dualism of either-or thinking.

"Should I quit my job, or stay and be miserable until I retire?" "Should we take a vacation or invest the money?" "Should I order a banana split with everything on it or skip dessert?" are all examples of dualistic thinking.

When we get stuck here, it is time to look for the third, fourth, and even fifth options. Here are only a few possibilities: "Maybe I could drop to half time at my job, while I develop a home-based business or consulting practice, or look at flex-time or job-sharing options." "Maybe we could go on a less expensive vacation and invest the leftover money, or have a vacation at home and be tourists in the city." "Maybe I could order the light dessert and enjoy it without feeling guilty, or plan a nice long walk or bike ride after the meal to compensate for my indulgence."

Bouncing between two (often equally dismal) choices can lead you to inaction at best and clinical depression at worst. It invites the martyr or victim to emerge, and it is almost impossible to see clearly or make positive choices while playing *those* roles.

Routine

We do not always look for the third option, because we get comfortable (or comfortably *un*comfortable) in routine. Sometimes we stop making new discoveries or showing up, because we are numbed by routine. We follow the same procedures (though inefficient or outdated), hold meetings at the same location (though uninspiring), and attend the same conventions each year (though they rarely provide useful information). Routine is not inherently negative. It blocks us, however, when we hang on to it for comfort. We choose not to do things differently, because venturing into the unknown could lead to feeling out of control or letting go of our familiar ways.

We all know what happens to our significant relationships when we stop making new discoveries. They stagnate and eventually die from lack of attention. As soon as we decide that we have learned everything there is to learn about someone and that there are no more surprises, an amazing thing happens: we stop learning new things about the person and we are no longer surprised! Ironically, we settle into the comfort of expecting things to be the same, and then become restless when they continue to be the same.

The same thing can happen in our work. We find our comfort zone and lose a sense of wonder and possibility. Unfortunately, the surprises are happening all around us, but we will not see them if we are not looking. If you're caught in this trap, it's time to consider doing things differently.

| DOING THINGS DIFFERENTLY |

Take Your Time

Counter the influence of the learned blocks with the principle *Show Up and Pay Attention*. We cannot make new discoveries without paying attention, and we cannot pay attention if we haven't first shown up. Once you arrive, take your time. I know, I know . . . here I go contradicting myself again. After busting the myth that time is essential for creativity, I'm asking you to take your time. Make some more room in your brain; both are true. While creative breakthroughs often happen on the fly—the "Aha!" inspired by the chance meeting or cross-pollination of previously unrelated ideas and objects—some insights and connections need nothing but time and easy attention to reveal themselves.

Holly Shulman, senior vp, group creative director at Frankel & Company, regularly leads her troops through ideation sessions. While she is ultimately responsible for delivering innovative marketing ideas to her clients, she discourages starting with the end in mind. She encourages taking time whenever possible:

Business expectations can suck the life out of creative collaboration. Discovery happens by relaxing and shifting from work to play. That can be difficult when there is pressure to justify all of those billable hours, but it's necessary if we are going to reach beyond the obvious. I try to make brainstorming more of an exploration than a problem-solving session. Otherwise it's tempting to go for the first thing that looks like a good idea. You can go just a little beyond the obvious and trick yourself into thinking you're being creative.

Einstein put time into the equation and came up with relativity theory. In business, we resist varying from time constraints. It is invariant, nonnegotiable. Or is it? In all things quantum and all processes creative there are options. *Take* more time when you can. *Make* more time when you can. When you can't change the quantity of time, change your *relationship* to time. When you are present in this moment, you are present in all possibilities. Time expands when you *Show Up and Pay Attention*, remember to breathe, be in the present moment, open your eyes, relax, and be willing to be surprised. Five minutes of all possibilities is worth five hours of stagnation.

A culture that supports discovery goes a long way, too. World cultures are often identified through their language, arts, and customs. Business cultures aren't far removed; they are identified by their beliefs and behaviors. Throughout the book I've discussed (hammered) the point that alignment of organizational values to daily practice is crucial to fostering workplace creativity.

Cultivate a Culture of Curiosity

While I point at the ugly creativity-killing organization, I *speak* to you, the hopeful reader in search of a way to breathe new life into your work. And you *should* be hopeful. You have more power than you know. Even you can cultivate a culture of curiosity. Cultivating a personal and organizational culture of curiosity is a wonderful way to combat the learned fear of looking stupid. Let everyone around you know that questions, especially dumb questions, are not only OK, but expected.

A manager shared her technique: whenever she hires a new employee, she asks them to come to her with at least five questions each day for the first month. Not only is this a wonderful way to establish communication, it teaches the new worker to look for and pursue the questions.

Why wait for an enlightened boss to create such a culture? You can give yourself the same assignment. Look for and ask at least five questions a day. Ask questions of the dictionary, your mail carrier, an on-line resource, the local library, a stranger at a stoplight, the newspaper, your children, or (let's not forget this resource) your Essence.

Collaborate and Separate

This all sounds good. After all, hierarchies are out, teams are in. Yes, *and* . . . beware of allowing team culture to rob you of necessary quiet time. Collaborate and separate. Collaboration is not exclusive of contemplation and individual exploration. Like a gigantic lung that expands and contracts, your separateness will breathe air into the togetherness. Likewise, togetherness in-spires your separateness. As a writer, I am an enthusiastic collaborator. If not formally cocreating a project, I seek out collaborative energy. I converse with clients, coffee with colleagues, kibitz with the neighbor kids, then separate to exhale my full creative lungs out onto the page.

Be Unrewarding

Like many artists and writers I know, I sometimes experience the road to be unrewarding, until I remember to be unrewarding. When you work conditionally, with an expectation that at the end (of the day, week, project) comes your booty, you cannot transcend to the infinite nuclear power of creativity. As with the corporate suggestion system, flawed by its well-intentioned cost-benefit associated rewards, you will only skim the surface of creative possibility—treading water to keep the carrot in view, instead of diving deep in search of sunken treasure.

My counsel is for you to not work for carrots, or any other dangling item sufficient to get your attention, but allow discovery itself to be your reward. Like the *kaizen teian* practitioners who several times a year happily cash their $3.33 checks for participating in their company's creativity initiatives, you must find your way back to the pleasure of the process.

Rewards are a touchy subject for my clients who find sales-driven bonus systems not only effective motivators, but expected incentives affecting both recruitment and retention of talented employees. Different animals. What motivates people to action can actually be detrimental to creativity (a process we know defies prescription). A horse may run faster in pursuit of a carrot, but will the carrot motivate him to come up with ideas for improving his training regime? Will the carrot make the ideas come faster? Will the ideas be more plentiful and innovative? (OK, so the analogy broke down, but you get the point).

Wonder

Not only will external rewards inhibit discovery, they can destroy wonder. Remember wonder? What did it feel like to go to the circus or a magic show and be in awe? Remember floating in questions? "How'd they do that?" "What happened to the rabbit?" "Did the woman *really* get sawed in half?" Wonder leaves you room for the possibility of magic—that something is possible completely outside of your realm of understanding or belief system. Aah! Now that is a lively awareness of possibilities!

Magicians are in the wonder business. They know the value of the feeling they create through their illusions. It's so valuable that they pay thousands for the most awesome illusions; so valuable that most of their secrets will follow them to their graves. If it's so valuable, there must be something in it for you. Give yourself the gift of wonder every chance you can. Besides catching the next magic show in town, you can do anything that gives you pause: read about the mysteries of quantum physics, science fiction, or childbirth; watch the gravity-defying leaps of ballet or the simplicity and power of waves washing to shore. Wonder is awe. It requires a generous serving of humility to enjoy. Be humble and you will be wonder-full. Then you will want to participate.

Participate

The creative process is an open system, demanding participation to transform. Modern physics made the shocking discovery that, at least at the subatomic level, the scientist participates in the scientific phenomenon. He influences that which he observes simply by observing it. No longer can the illusion of the detached observer or of independent parts exist. Neither can you isolate yourself from the living system in which you work. In participation you affect transformation. You cannot observe its unfolding; you must participate. You must make new discoveries during each twist and turn or transformation will not evolve. Sure, change will happen even if you hide under your desk. *Growth* happens with discovery and discovery with participation.

Be Sensual

"When you are in a creative mode, all of your senses want to be involved," Shulman reports. Ideation sessions are often outfitted with piles of playthings: squishy balls, slinkys, soap bubbles, clay, flying objects, and more. Images on the walls and music also encourage participants to tap into their whole being, to stimulate unusual connections, and explore possibilities.

Your office needn't compete with FAO Schwartz to enliven your senses. In discovery mode, even the most familiar and unassuming environment yields infinite information. To demonstrate this, I send my students off to make at least three new discoveries about a familiar person, place, and object. When they return, they are surprised to find they couldn't stop at just three things. Suddenly their beige workstation comes alive, their spouse of twenty years reveals new qualities, the keyboard, hair dryer, or blender is new again—even otherworldly—seen with discovering eyes. This is only a start, of course. Think of it as "discovery yoga," a lifelong practice of building flexibility and stamina to be sensual in each aspect of your work.

Change Your Point of View

While you are practicing, you may find it helpful to change your point of view. Especially if all you see is what you've always seen. Like Kurasawa's *Rashomon*, a cinematic tale told from three different character's perspectives, your story will seem entirely new from a fresh angle. Spend an hour in your boss's shoes (or those of your employee, child, student, customer, teacher, or even your pet—OK, pets don't wear shoes, but you get the idea).

Shulman challenges herself to change her point of view when developing promotion ideas for familiar products:

> *We've all grown up with certain brand names and products. Sometimes it's hard to see them in a new light, let alone to get consumers to do the same. So I like to change my perspective using a completely unrelated product. For example, if we are working on a cosmetics promotion, I might think about cars. "How do car*

companies get people excited about their product? What does a 'test drive' look like at the make-up counter?" Suddenly we are seeing our assignment for the first time.

The awakening that comes with "the first time" jump-starts our desire to *Make Continuous Discoveries*. You can change your point of view anytime you want. Take a different route to work or ride your bike in a new neighborhood. Take a day trip to someplace you have never been. (In most big cities you only need to go several blocks to experience a completely different culture). Eat at a new restaurant, shop at a different grocery store, get lost at a street fair, or just get lost!

Perhaps this is what French director Jacques Copeau had in mind when he developed a rehearsal technique to help his actors find new layers to their characters and the story. He asked the actors to put aside their scripts and improvise the story, starting with movement only, then adding character, setting, and dialogue.[4] Without lines, the actors were free to concentrate on their characters, the story, and the relationships on stage. They also had no difficulty creating the "illusion of the first time," because it was!

One of my students, inspired by Jacques Copeau, revisited a long-buried passion. As a child she had a natural affinity for sewing and loved to create her own patterns. In high school her enthusiasm was soon squelched by a demanding teacher, who made it clear that there was only one right way to sew and my student was not doing it that one way. Soon she lost interest in sewing altogether and for years did not return to it—until she heard of Jacques Copeau.

She bought a pattern for a hat that would be perfect to wear to an upcoming wedding. She took out the pattern and spent a few minutes studying it. She then tossed it aside, sketched her own, and proceeded to cut and sew as she once loved to do as a young woman. She glowed when she brought her hat to class. It (and she) was stunning. She reawakened her creativity by changing her point of view.

Celebrate Foolishness

She also let herself celebrate foolishness. Throughout history fools have filled an important need. Society has granted court jesters, traveling players, clowns, stand-up comics, cartoonists, and improvisers license to comment on, tease, cajole, and "fool" us out of our perceptions and into questioning the status quo. To accomplish this they often play the fool, the simpleton, the braggart, the curmudgeon, the baffoon, the miser, the cad, or the hopeless romantic. These "social workers" have traditionally not come under the same censorious scrutiny as the rest of us (except in severely repressed cultures). We give them the same leeway we give children and, as children do, they help us see the folly of our ways. By making fools of *them*selves, they allow us to recognize our own foolishness and humanity.

Interesting, but how is that going to help you transform the way you work? Paul Birch at British Airways donned the title of Corporate Jester. His role was "to declare 'Just because you're the boss, doesn't mean you know better.' . . . to stir things up."[5] You may not get approval to put *fool* on your business card, but you can approve of foolishness and the space it creates for possibility.

Fools help us see things differently, the first step toward *doing* things differently. When we risk being foolish, we not only risk seeing things differently, we risk sharing laughter with others, revealing our cherished human qualities, deepening our spirituality, learning from our mistakes, discovering more possibilities, and having creative breakthroughs. (Now, what was it we were afraid of?)

Discovery may not lead you to play with washcloths at Japanese restaurants or write stand-up routines. And however and whenever we practice it, discovery will bring a wealth of creative energy and a renewed sense of wonder. Here you may find yourself not only doing things differently, but doing *different* things.

1. Holton.
2. Kleinman.
3. Jones. Roundabout Theatre Company Home Page.
4. Frost and Yarrow, 22.
5. Sittenfeld, 66.

The Boundaries: Five University of Central Florida film school graduates. One 16-mm camera. One Hi-8 video camera. One digital sound recorder. Three actors. Eight days in Maryland's Seneca Creek State Park. $30,000.00.

The Freedom: Eight days of improvisation in the woods with the actors as camera operators whose assignment was to "document the legend of the Blair Witch." Each day they were directed to a new location via handheld Global Positioning System devices where they found canisters of film, supplies, and their acting assignment for the day (none of the actors were privy to the other's directions).

At the end of the eight days, the filmmakers edited together the collected footage, deciding against any additional background story or commentary, aside from a cryptic opening statement. Viewers were told that they were about to see the footage found from three student filmmakers, Heather Donahue, Joshua Leonard, and Michael Williams, who hiked into the Black Forest of Maryland to shoot a documentary film on a local legend called the "Blair Witch" and were never seen or heard from again.

A year before the film's debut, the producers launched a website dedicated to the mythology of the Blair Witch. It received millions of hits before *The Blair Witch Project* premiered in January 1999 at a midnight screening during the Sundance Film Festival. At press time, the "crew" was unavailable for comment (they were missing, after all). The buzz was deafening.

In an age where young filmmakers bemoan the impossibility of raising the millions needed for the most modest of films, Haxan Films found a way not just to "get the job done," but to use the limitations to their advantage. "We took pretty much just every limitation that independent, low-budget films have, and used it as our strength. Shaky camera, no lights, improvised dialog . . ." said codirector and cowriter, Eduardo Sánchez.

ALLOW THE BOUNDARIES TO FREE YOU

Encounter Unlimited
Possibilities Within the Limits

| **THE PRINCIPLE** | This is just the beginning of the story. By the morning after the film's premiere, Artisan Entertainment had won the bidding war, laying down one million dollars for distribution rights. By the summer of 1999, it was one of the hottest films of the season, making $1.5 million on its opening weekend while showing at only twenty six screens, and mushrooming to $50 million at the box office on its first wide-release weekend. Soon the cast (who emerged to enjoy their success) and filmmakers had made the talk-show rounds and signed mega-deals for more projects.

Couldn't happen in your industry? Couldn't happen to you? Couldn't happen to Steve Jobs of Apple, who started by tinkering in his garage; Sam Walton of Wal-Mart, who started with his single store; or to the 65-year-old Colonel Harland Sanders with his $105 social security check investment and secret recipe? Couldn't happen to a young woman named Oprah from Kosciusko, Mississippi? Of course it can't happen—until it *does* happen. Until someone makes the quantum leap and discovers her- or himself in a new place filled with possibility. *Allow the Boundaries to Free You* is the last principle of Quantum Creativity because it describes the divine alchemy of all the principles, fueled to discovery by passion and channeled through boundaries. Just as the raging river gains strength and power as it passes through canyons and is cradled by its banks until it eventually finds freedom in a larger body of water, your creativity can be propelled by the boundaries through which it flows into a reservoir of possibilities.

The Givens

Boundaries guide rather than impede progress. In theatrical improvisation, boundaries are called givens—skeletal information needed to start a scene, such as "who," "what," and "where." In improvisation the givens may come from audience suggestions of a phrase, theme, or topic. Once these parameters are set, the improvisers are free to make continuous discoveries within these limits. Together they create fanciful realities, are transported onto faraway planets, the distant future, the dusty past, and inside their fellow players' minds. They transform into a variety of characters; take on and discard accents, physical limitations, and disabilities; morph into animals, inanimate objects, natural elements; and more.

When any one of the players denies the givens—contributions made by the audience or fellow players—the scene gets bogged down and confused (remember George's experience with the boat?). Struggling against the givens in improvisation has the same effect as saying no. It wastes creative energy, stopping progress in its tracks. The same thing happens in your collaborations: discovery stops when the agreed-upon boundaries are denied. Struggling against "what is" also drains valuable potential energy and inhibits creative leaping.

We all have givens in our lives, boundaries that can either restrict or channel creativity, depending on our relationship to them. For some, time is an effective facilitator: two days to finish the proposal, five months to plan the wedding, three weeks to rehearse the show, etc. Money is often a boundary; launching a new marketing campaign, rehabbing a kitchen, or getting an education may be bound by funds. Available staff is a boundary for many, especially with the leaner-meaner trend set in motion the nineties, coupled with low unemployment rates. Transforming the way you work is not about working harder (you are already tap-dancing as fast as you can), but about working *easier*. Allow the boundaries to support you.

Accept the Boundaries

My high school drama coach used to gather her overly made-up troupe for a preperformance warm-up chant: "Faster! Funnier! Louder!" we cheered several times, before heading toward the auditorium wings to make our first entrances. This may have focused our teenage energy and built some team spirit, but it certainly isn't where I would start if I wanted my ensemble to show up with their whole selves to cocreate an engaging event for the audience.

You may have heard echoes of this cheer at your workplace. "Faster! Smarter! More creative!" it barks. Unlike the drama coach who starts with the end in mind, you will achieve these qualities by letting go of them when you *Allow the Boundaries to Free You*, rather than making the boundaries succumb to your will. Sometimes it is easier to see how this is possible in someone else's work, than to notice the opportunity for freedom in your own.

Some years ago a woman appeared in a creativity group I was coleading. Amy was exhausted and starved for what the group had to offer. She had recently given birth to her second child, a boy with

Down's syndrome. Although a trained concert pianist, Amy was having difficulty finding time to brush her teeth, let alone to express her creativity. Nonetheless, she managed to carve out one Saturday afternoon each week to participate in the group.

For the first few weeks, the group listened to Amy as she shared her struggles and discoveries. Members became increasingly uncomfortable, however, as they detected her growing resentment toward those who did not have her responsibilities. "You don't understand!" she would say. "I *can't* find time for myself with kids around every minute of the day." They gently supported her while also telling her that they didn't believe her excuses and looked forward to seeing her the following week. The group wasn't buying the con that she was helpless.

Several months later Amy arrived radiant. She couldn't wait to share her news. After months of struggling *against* her responsibilities, Amy finally accepted them as boundaries and found ways to work within them. She traded child care with a neighbor and found a nonprofit agency that provided respite workers to give parents of disabled children a break. With her newfound freedom, Amy had made time to play the piano again and design a Halloween costume for her older son.

Today Amy (now the mother of four boys) is one of the most creative people I know. She actively participates in the PTA, volunteers for a community newsletter, speaks regularly at conferences, and finds time to play the piano, sew costumes, and decorate cakes in the shape of trains, cowboy boots, and houses—all by accepting the boundaries in her life and playing within them. She reflected:

> *Making time for myself has required some changing of priorities in our household (but no one seems to mind—it was a much bigger deal for me). What has been really fulfilling is my family's response to me when I do take time for myself. Because I feel better, they feel better.*

Whenever I feel overwhelmed and victimized by my responsibilities and schedule, I think of Amy. She inspires me, reminding me that I have choices; if she can do it, I, too, can allow the boundaries to free me. So can you. No more excuses.

As with most Quantum Creativity principles, this one is intimately connected to another. Before we can *allow* the boundaries to free us, we must *accept* them; we must say, "Yes, and . . ." to them. "Yes" is acceptance. "And . . ." is freedom—the play of possibilities within boundaries. Holly Shulman says, "If you give up your resistance to boundaries, you make room for innovative solutions."

Recovery

Like the producers of *The Blair Witch Project*, when we acknowledge what is, we can use it to our advantage. This is not unlike the addict's journey through early recovery. Abstinence begins with defining and accepting the boundaries that ultimately free the individual from the grip of addiction. With substance addiction, this journey starts with not using the substance. Simple—not easy.

Abstinence from process addictions (in which the process itself is the fix) is not so clear-cut. A compulsive spender cannot simply stop using money, but must define an abstinent spending plan. This plan is not meant to be a restrictive budget, but a clear set of boundaries within which the addict can enjoy abundance. The same holds true for all potentially addictive processes—relationships, exercise, sex, eating, work, etc. It is not necessary to stop participating in these processes altogether, but to define healthy relationships to them. Abstinence or the set of boundaries that offers liberation will be different for each individual. Here, too, there are no prescriptions.

Many mistake the struggle to find freedom within boundaries for a personal battle of will. You may have heard dieters and smokers talk of their struggles to find necessary willpower and discipline.

They believe that therein lies the secret to their success. Not mustering enough of it can only reflect some deep-seated weakness of character. It's not true. Freedom from the bonds of addiction has nothing to do with these convictions.

Workplace stagnation is not so far removed from addiction. In fact, the underlying process is often indistinguishable and the results are the same—disconnection from essential purpose, passion, and creativity. Like the addict, we can create much unnecessary suffering for ourselves when we struggle against what is, rather than simply define the boundaries within which we will find freedom. Acceptance of boundaries, whether in our personal lives or at work, creates space for transformation.

It may seem odd to refer to addiction in the context of transformation. My intention is not to enlarge the volumes of literature on the subject, but to use it to illuminate your understanding of freedom within boundaries. When you accept the givens, you lay the foundation for creative possibilities. Soon the boundaries become incidental; the focus shifts from limitation to freedom.

Fast-growing organizations have to distinguish between boundaries and limitations. When the two are confused, resources are drained. Success lies in clarity. Qwest Communications International, Inc. is building a high-capacity Internet-based fiber-optic network under the leadership of chairman and CEO, Joseph Nacchio.

> *When you're trying to make a big play in a space that remains undefined . . . the leader's job is to make sure that all people in your organization understand where they can work autonomously and where they must collaborate. . . . My job is recognizing what needs structure and what doesn't.*[1]

Clarifying boundaries is the first step toward freedom for both the individual and the organization. Many of the companies I work with to find innovative business solutions are surprised to find that their first order of business is to improve communication. Frustration levels run high when people don't know where to take their ideas and, if they do share their ideas, they often wonder whatever happened to the ideas, how they follow up, and who they can count on to champion innovation. Once the channels are clarified, creativity is free to flow unimpeded.

Does *Allow the Boundaries to Free You* counter the popular creativity notions encouraging us to "think out of the box," *break* boundaries, and push past limitations? Not at all. In fact, we stay in our boxes when we battle against the few nonnegotiable limitations. Freedom arrives on the wings of acceptance. Often we miss the opportunities *within* boundaries, because of a final set of learned blocks.

| LEARNED BLOCKS |

Limits Are Limiting

Just as we learned to look for the flaws in emerging ideas, we have an uncanny knack for seeing the reasons why something *can't* be done: There is not enough staff to improve productivity. Technology is changing too quickly for us to keep up. The advertising budget has been spent; there's nothing left to promote new product features. It is so tempting, and way too easy, to build a case for stagnation from the evidence of limitations.

Unlimited resources are *not* the key to creativity. On the contrary, they can actually be disadvantageous. William Rutter, chairman of Chiron Technologies, a successful biotechnology corporation, observes:

> . . . *all abundant resources do is allow you to think creatively about how to spend resources . . . which diverts you from doing the actual research. You develop new programs, build big laboratories, and pretty soon, instead of solving problems in the present, you are just banking on the future.*[2]

Oddly enough, abundant resources can distract from possibilities. Boundaries of time and money may help reveal the simplest, most efficient solution. Unless, of course, you choose to wallow in *"If only . . ."*

If Only . . .

If only I had more money to hire additional staff, buy a new computer, go back to school . . . " "If only I had time to get in shape, take that watercolor class, vacation . . ." It is amazing how many excuses we find for not living creative, fulfilling lives. "Sure, it's easy for so-and-so," we tell ourselves, "He doesn't have kids, my job, an elderly parent," etc.

When we blame others or our circumstances at work or at home, we are victims, helpless to choose or change at all. This worldview is limiting. When we accept the boundaries, we have choices again. We are no longer victims of circumstance.

No Time

Equally debilitating is the belief that only people with a lot of time on their hands can be creative. This variation on the earlier learned block, "Chaos wastes time," is a favorite for many of us. I hear it repeated again and again in corporations: "I'm so busy responding to E-mail, returning calls, attending meetings, and responding to crises. I don't have time to be creative!" Indeed. In an age where the Internet has given us terms like *time zero* and an intolerance for even the slightest delay, time is a hotter commodity than ever.

More than once in these pages, I have raised the subject of time and workplace creativity. I have made cases for both taking your time and not letting the lack of it constrain you. Again, both are true. Paradox and contradiction are, after all, in abundance in the quantum world and in your creative life.

By naming time as a boundary you have the opportunity to find freedom within it; you can change your relationship to time, rather than battle against its lack. Within the boundaries of time you will be delivered to presence, to the place of discovery. In discovery, as in the quantum leap, time is transcended. I have never heard an improviser complain that she didn't have enough *time* to respond to her fellow player, or that she would have offered something more useful if only she hadn't felt so rushed. I *have* heard improvisers say they "didn't feel all there" during the performance, and apologize for not being more available on stage. Time is never the issue; presence is.

Presence leads to acceptance of the nonnegotiable, and awareness of the possibilities therein. Those who transform the way they work discover that the best way to save time is to stop doing what doesn't work. Most people can name a few things that do not work at work. It may be the petty cash approval process, technology training, or the meetings, meetings, meetings. While petty cash, training and meetings may all be necessary, within those boundaries there are many possibilities. For starters, petty cash approval can be simplified, training options broadened, and meetings made more efficient (and fun!)—all within your givens. By applying the other principles of Quantum Creativity (such as *Make Continuous Discoveries, Say, "Yes, And . . . ,"* and *Embrace Chaos*) you can find new ways to accomplish the things that are not working now. You can begin doing things differently.

| DOING THINGS DIFFERENTLY |

Name the Givens

Confusion quickly gives way to clarity when we Name the Givens. While improvisers never plan their performances (or it wouldn't be improvisation), they will take a moment to be sure everyone understands the givens. These may have come from the audience, a current event, or a random drawing. As soon as all of the players are in agreement on the nonnegotiable givens ("Did he say 'flat top' or 'fat cop?'"), they can play, discovering endless possibilities as they heighten and explore within the boundaries.

I have never seen so much confusion on stage *or* in the workplace as when there was no shared understanding and acceptance of the givens. One third of the team is sure they heard "fat cop," another third is playing with "flat top," and the remaining players are denying both. This is not chaos (there is no vision or self-organization here). This is pain. This is _____. (You may have an even stronger word, one that my publisher would rather I not use, but you can fill in the blank if you need to vent). However you describe it, the outcome is the same. When you are vague about the boundaries, or fight them, you cannot be freed by them.

Start where improvisers start. Name what you cannot change. Identify and clarify your givens, your nonnegotiables. Time, budget, staff, and client expectations are just a few. It is dangerous to assume agreement without discussion. A small investment here will prevent a big one down the road.

It is also worth scrutinizing the boundaries before you name them as such. Are you unconsciously stalled by obstacles that don't exist? Or perhaps you are naming the *wrong* boundary. Remember my struggle with the decision to sell my beloved suv? For months all I could see was the boundary of "I need transportation." To me, transportation equaled owning a car. Challenging that assumption freed me to explore other options within my true boundary: I needed transportation. Soon I was freed from the expense, responsibility, and time consumed by owning a car (just finding parking could eat up forty-five minutes a day). A whole new frontier of rental cars, public transportation, walking, and cycling unfurled before me. More time, less stress, and better health filled the empty (parking) space. Limitations lay only in mistaking boundaries for barriers.

Once you start looking, it is easy to define these tangible day-to-day boundaries. It can be difficult, however, to define another, perhaps more illusive, boundary that can facilitate a deep level of creative freedom. You need to articulate your vision.

Articulate Your Vision

Like the strange attractors of chaos theory that describe self-organizing patterns within constant change, your vision gives continuity to creativity, allowing great freedom and exploration within the bounds of your dream. Vision provides a guiding force or framework within which you access infinite possibility. If you take the time to discover your vision, then your boundaries, your givens, the possibilities become, paradoxically, bound*less*. Each member of a collaborative team may have different ideas of *how* to achieve the vision, yet the group creative process may yield something altogether different. There need not be a conflict here. Accepted vision allows individuals to transcend their differences. Chaos tends toward order without denying creativity.

Values and philosophy also serve as guiding or self-organizing forces. In organizations, consensus and acceptance of the vision and its embedded values are paramount. Of course, there must *be* a vision. I sometimes consult with nonprofit organizations writing their mission statement, trying to define their purpose. They are establishing boundaries. With a strong sense of purpose, an organization can readily enlist support. Without one, members lose focus and morale suffers.

Certainly, as with all things living and creative, the vision need not be etched in stone. It will evolve and change over time. Every member's participation in that development process ensures ownership of and commitment to the vision. Everyone in the organization needs to work within the same boundaries, within the same set of givens. To use another improvisation metaphor, if I'm standing at a bus stop and you're stuck in an elevator, we might have a difficult time getting our scene off the ground.

One of my favorite vision statements grew out of a lively collaboration Rick Walters had with his managers and associates at Automatic Data Processing:

> *To be renowned for inspired associates providing legendary service with a spirit of community in a fun, excitovating environment.*

Rick and his team weren't even stalled by the limits of the English language. When they couldn't find a word to describe their vision for a dynamic work environment, they created a new one. ADP takes seriously its mission to be "the employer of choice" in its industry. Only through attracting and retaining the best and brightest can they fulfill their goal, as they have done for 150 consecutive quarters (as of this writing), to be the "vendor of choice."

Organizations may choose to create additional boundaries to keep their energy focused. For example, the lofty vision "to end world hunger," will be a difficult self-organizer, an unclear given, without some early boundaries. The organization may refine the mission: "to end world hunger through community-based agricultural programs." These specifics channel creative energy. As long as the vision leads, additional boundaries will line up to support its realization.

You do not need to have a global vision to improve the quality of life for all humankind, in order to benefit from this principle. When you accept your vision as a given, all of your energy is naturally directed toward its achievement. In the presence of vision, you need not strive, control, or otherwise regulate your creative energy.

Are you having difficulty putting words to your vision and values—your personal mission statement? Grab a piece of paper, or find some white space in this book, and make a list in answer to this question: "What am I most proud of?" Write down anything that matters to you—accomplishments, personal attributes, compliments you've received. Then walk away. Give your list some breathing room. When you return, it will tell you something about the person who wrote it. It will tell you what is meaningful to that person. It will lead you to vision, to your operating principles.

This question is also one of the simplest ways I know to assess personal and organizational alignment. After I read my clients' corporate literature and interview workers throughout their organizations, I will return to the executives and ask them individually what they are most proud of. When the mission trumpets service and customer satisfaction, and VPs rattle off profit margins, stock prices, and market share without the slightest reference to the glossy corporate values, I know we have some work to do. We have found an opportunity for freedom and innovation. If you discover a similar discontinuity between the values you espouse and your responses to the "pride question," you, too, have hit pay dirt. You now have an opportunity to align your life and your work with all that you find meaningful.

Are you proud of the challenges you have met? Seek out more challenge in your work. Are you proud of the wonderful environment you have fostered in the workplace? Share your ideas with others. Are you proud of your family? Look for opportunities to increase your participation. Now you are onto something!

Create More Boundaries

Your vision will light your way, when there is little else to guide you. With all of this illumination, you may find yourself enthused with passion, full of vision, *and* completely overwhelmed with the enormity of it all. In this wonderful, terrifying, paralyzing place create more boundaries.

I find it difficult to begin large creative projects (developing a new show, designing a course, or writing this book, for example) without defining specific boundaries. This might be as simple as making a to-do list for the day, or as elaborate as detailing a work plan with deadlines for each stage of the process. Within these givens, I relax. I am in good hands. I am in my private creativity spa. I am not in charge. I do not have to fight or force. The door is open, the ideas will come (eventually).

Establishing and honoring boundaries has nothing to do with discipline. Banish this word from your creativity lexicon. It does not take discipline or self-will to *Allow the Boundaries to Free You*. It does not take any more discipline to meditate, exercise, and write each day than it does to brush your teeth. "Yeah, right," you say. It sounds outrageous—and it's true. I learned long ago, as a teenage student of meditation, that freedom came, not with my practice of meditation, but with my relationship to the practice. If I awoke each morning ready to debate whether or not I felt like meditating and tried to rationalize my way to another half hour's sleep, I would be drained for the rest of the day (whether or not I actually meditated). As soon as I changed my relationship to the boundary, the daily debates stopped. When I aligned myself with my values, I eliminated the need for discipline. You will find the same freedom within the boundaries of your vision.

Allow the Boundaries to Free You is deeply interconnected with the other Quantum Creativity principles. Any boundary is a barricade if we do not have a healthy relationship to it (e.g., a budget or diet seems punitive, while a spending or food plan offers hope and freedom). When we show up and pay attention, we may discover that our original vision and boundaries are no longer appropriate. When we make continuous discoveries and embrace chaos, we will be able to name the new boundaries as they are needed. Intuition, passion, acceptance, and trust are all touchstones along the way to freedom. Without them, our commitment to creativity reduces to yet another set of rules and regulations that characterize the mechanistic system stifling us in the first place. Within the boundaries, freedom and joy are abundant. Filmmakers make groundbreaking debuts, scientists make breakthrough discoveries, and overwhelmed parents find time to nurture themselves, as well as their children.

———————

1. Nacchio, 98.
2. Perry, 16.

TRANSFORMING

Embracing a new way of working is not like shifting gears on a sports car or changing hairstyles. Transformation is a process, not an event. Like all processes, as we have seen, it is filled with the unexpected: chaos, gifts, frustration, wonder, and, ultimately, immense growth, power, and freedom. If you have read this book in search of a prescription for creativity, I hope you have been disappointed—and inspired. Like a good party, best enjoyed when you bring your whole wonderful self without expectation or agenda, you and your work will transform as you participate and allow the conversations and events to unfold.

Throughout these pages I have referred to the seemingly unrelated art of improvisation, quantum physics, and even recovery from addiction; all in the service of shedding light on transformation and, specifically, to support you in transforming the way you work.

Though incongruent at first glance, you have seen their commonality. Improv players step up to transform and be transformed as they channel and receive collaborative energy. Quantum physics teaches that the observer is also a participant in what is observed. And those seeking freedom from addiction learn to get out of the way of transformation as they identify the boundaries for recovery. In each case, participation fosters transformation. Paradoxically, doing things differently requires little actual *doing* and much more *being*. Present participation always leads to transformation.

Simple—not easy. I wouldn't dare share these ideas with you if I didn't practice them (oh so imperfectly) myself. While I have shared a number of hard-won lessons from my work over the years, my journey continues. In transforming the way I work and in writing this book, I have been challenged to *listen, follow, abstain, say yes, trust, embrace, show up, discover,* and *allow.* Each principle gave me faith and courage as I faced my piles of notes; rejection slips; deadlines; the blank computer screen; feedback from friends, colleagues, and editors; and rewrite after rewrite after rewrite.

When I step back from the details of the process, the up-close-and-personal minutiae of my life and work, I see the process as well as the *process* of the process. With distance I can see the sometimes imperceptible shifting of the tectonic plates of beliefs and behaviors—of my personal paradigm. Though I knew something important was in motion, I didn't quite know how to describe it, until I reflected on something a friend shared with me some years ago. It's from a section of the "big book" of Alcoholics Anonymous known as "the promises" and reads, in part, "Fear of economic insecurity will leave you." When I first heard of it, I thought it was a ridiculous promise to make to members of a group charged with supporting recovery from addiction. How could they possibly peer into a global crystal ball and promise such a thing? How could they foresee the twists and turns in each individual member's life and proclaim an absence of economic insecurity? And what was a statement like that doing in the text of a supposedly spiritual program, anyway?

Years later I found myself reflecting on this promise and I "got it." The promise does not predict the outcome. It is not some rosy rags-to-riches proclamation. It is a promise of restoration to the *process*. A promise that with a commitment to live a life of purpose and presence, "*Fear* . . . will leave you." Without fear, possibilities are boundless, horizons vast, and freedom infinite. That is the promise of transformation.

It is also wonderful and infuriating that even *that* promise is not an outcome. It can only be fulfilled through simple, daily commitment. If you happen to be human, daily commitment will be an imperfect practice. You will be challenged along the way. And, like the serpents and Sirens that the heroes of Greek mythology battled, obstacles are a sure sign that you are onto something big. Perhaps the notes that follow will be useful when you wake up in the middle of the night certain that your passion will lead to ruin and humiliation or that your misgivings signal you took a wrong turn somewhere.

When you feel that you have forgotten everything you once knew, take a moment. Release your grip. Breathe. Be gentle. Go to your silence or what you know to be Essential. Rest there for a while. While you are finding your way back home, take heart in these few simple truths.

| PAIN IS NOT A REASON TO GIVE UP |

Pain reminds you that you are alive. Sometimes you will lose, almost everything, perhaps. You will fall, hard. You will fail, miserably. You will make mistakes—big stinky ones. You will feel hurt, more than you ever knew you could. You will cause others pain—oh, will you cause pain! And you will forget past lessons, as if you never learned them. This is all part of the adventure.

And you will get up again, look around, take stock of what you learned, perhaps make a few amends, reset your course, and be on your way, sometimes making it up as you go along, . . . *and* you will get there. You will get to your full, messy, passionate, loving life.

| DEVOTION, DEVOTION, DEVOTION |

Do not shortchange yourself from the freedom and power of one-pointed commitment to purpose—persistence of vision. Allow the boundaries of your dreams to set you free in a world of infinite possibilities. Without doubt, your actions will be full of expectant energy, energy that *expects* success and fulfillment. Maharishi Mahesh Yogi was fond of saying, "Just pick something great and do it." Simple.

Your greatness may come to you through devotion to a spiritual practice, a committed partnership, physical fitness, your children, your community, your artistic vision, or a business venture. It does not matter. Value your time and presence enough to give it a clear channel, then stand back! Anything is possible now.

| THE PATH OF ESSENCE IS NOT THE EASY PATH |

The path of Essence requires letting go, commitment, patience, and a level of intimacy with yourself that can be downright unsettling.

The rewards, however, are immense. I hope the stories throughout this book give you faith and knowledge that a creative life is not a magical city reserved only for the privileged royalty we call artists or inventors. Of course, it is not a destination at all.

| BEWARE OF THE DOGMA |

As soon as you think you have found *the* way, you are in trouble. You are no longer a seeker, but a follower. Follow *your* passion, not someone else's path. A friend or mentor's wisdom, religious, and spiritual traditions, even the Quantum Creativity principles can inspire you, enthuse you, but they cannot replace the universal subatomic power of your Essence. Most spiritual traditions have grown out of the cognitions of women and men who paid attention to the voice of spirit in whatever way it came to them. The traditions that emerged from these great seers and prophets help us find our way.

These teachings, however, hinder us when we forget that we must participate in them to bring them to life. As soon as another's truth becomes our dogma, we give up responsibility for our own path. So yes, read your Bible, Torah, Bhagavad Gita; go to your church, temple, meditation center; listen to your elders, mentors, and wise friends; and . . . listen to your silence, your heart, your higher power, your Essence.

| ENDURANCE |

"In Training for Life" reads the slogan for the Special Olympics. Aren't we all? It may take some time to build your stamina. Start by walking your creative spirit around the block; little by little increase your pace and distance. What was once a struggle will soon seem a natural part of your life. There is no substitute for mileage, no liposuction to clear away your creative blocks or catapult you into your fully realized vision, just the journey, the training run. It's all practice. And it all counts.

| SWAN DIVE INTO YOUR LIFE |

Let go to the free fall of being in love—the grace, the passion, the power of it. In love you are invincible. Your vision is invincible. Trust that success comes with letting go. The diver springs into the air, finds the proper angle, and surrenders. You are trained for this dive. You are ready to let go.

| LAUGH EARLY, LAUGH OFTEN |

We are so silly, we humans. We meet our demise when we think we are important—that it actually matters whether we wear the blue suit or the green suit, whether we order the Caesar salad or the baby back ribs, whether we take the job in Tucson or stay in scenic Peoria.

Call your friends in the middle of the night to talk about your latest symptoms of mental illness. Find friends who will yank you out of your spin cycle, the hamster wheel in your head. Please laugh. Morbid self-reflection is your undoing. Yes, know thyself, but do so in the world along with the rest of us bunglers. Come on in! The water is fine, and we all look goofy in these swimming suits.

| WHEN THE GOING GETS TOUGH, THE TOUGH SAY, "THANK YOU!" |

In the darkness of personal doubt, confusion, and apparent failure, the quickest way back to the light is gratitude. When things do not go as *I* planned, I rail at the universe, and the universe smiles back at me. If I notice the smile at all, I think it is a sarcastic smirk meaning, "Ha! Who did you think you were, anyway?" But when I open my eyes wide and take a look around, I see that the smile is a loving one casting light on all of the gifts in my life. My restoration begins by taking inventory of the basics (I have a roof over my head, food in the refrigerator; I have a refrigerator, loyal, irreverent friends, a love-bucket of a dog, meaningful work . . .), and then I move to the subtler riches (an afternoon spent walking through the cemetery; my friend's new baby squeezing my finger; the chill from a spring breeze; the sweet, tart taste of a Braeburn apple; a belly laugh with pals as we remember our past fiascos . . .).

At its simplest, gratitude boils down to acknowledging the at once grace*ful* and grace*less* gift of being human. Sometimes it hits me between the eyes and brings me to my knees. "Oh, I get it! I *get* to be here. I *get* to feel this pain, celebrate this joy, find my way in this darkness. Thank you, for trusting me with this gift!" With that remembrance comes humility. Get up again, gather your courage, forge ahead and then give it away.

| GIVE IT AWAY |

There is no holding on to the truly valuable gifts, the fruits of living a creative life: love, joy, passion, wisdom, and many others. At the same time, there is no losing these gifts if you give them away every chance you get. Share the universe's blessings with others; the blessings will boomerang back to you, often transformed by the recipient, and smack you on the back of the head. You will wake up again and again.

If you think you have nothing to share, get over yourself! Get out there. Teaching reminds you of what you know while demanding that you continue to learn. Teaching keeps you honest. Be a sage, a prophet. Share a smile, a chuckle. Join in, be human. Tell your story; listen to others'. Be silly and profound. Give it away or you will forget.

BIBLIOGRAPHY

Adler, Tony. "The How of Funny." *American Theatre*, December 1993.

Alcoholics Anonymous. New York: Alcoholics Anonymous World Services, 1976.

Capra, Fritjof. *The Tao of Physics*. Boston: Shambhala, 1991.

Courage to Change. New York: Al-anon Family Groups, 1992.

Crisis of Perception: Art Meets Science and Spirituality in a Changing Economy. New York: Mystic Fire Video, 1993.

Dickson, Paul. The Future File. (Rawson Associates)

Diller, Barry. "The Discomfort Zone." *Inc. Magazine*, November 1995.

Drucker, Peter. *Management Challenges for the 21st Century*. New York: HarperBusiness, 1999.

Hall, Nina, ed. *Exploring Chaos*. New York: W.W. Norton, 1994.

Fox, Matthew. *Creation Spirituality*. San Francisco; HarperSanFrancisco, 1991.

Frost, Anthony and Ralph Yarrow. *Improvisation in Drama*. New York: St. Martin's Press, 1989.

Gamow, George. *The Thirty Years That Shook Physics*. New York: Doubleday, 1966.

Gleick, James. *Chaos: Making a New Science*. New York: Viking, 1987.

Goldberg, Natalie. *Writing Down the Bones*. Boston: Shambhala, 1986.

Gribbin, John. *In Search of Schrödinger's Cat: Quantum Physics and Reality*. New York: Bantam Books, 1983.

Guest, Judith. "103 Tips from Bestselling Writers." *Writer's Digest*, July, 1997.

Halpern, Charna, Del Close, and Kim "Howard" Johnson. *Truth in Comedy*. Colorado Springs, CO: Meriwether, 1993.

Handy, Charles. *The Age of Unreason*. Cambridge, MA: Harvard Business School Press, 1990.

Hawkins, Jeff. *Fast Company Magazine*, June 1998.

Hazen, Robert M., and James Trefil. *Science Matters*. New York: Anchor Books, Doubleday, 1991.

Holton, Lisa. "Keeping It Current," *Chicago Tribune*. November 15, 1998.

Jones, Cherry. Interview. Roundabout Theatre Company Home Page, [http://www.roundabouttheatre.org/cherry.html]. On-line. Netscape, May 10, 1996.

Jones, Cherry. "Thoughts on Theatre: An Interview with John Glover and Cherry Jones." *Equity News*, September 1995.

Keeva, Steven. "Opening the Mind's Eye." *ABA Journal*. June, 1996.

Kleinman, Carol. *Chicago Tribune*. August 15, 1999.

Lamott, Anne. *Bird by Bird*. New York: Pantheon Books, 1994.

Lederman, Leon. *The God Particle*. New York: Dell Publishing, 1996.

Lerman, Liz. "Toward a Process for Critical Response." From *Alternate Roots*, a publication of the Regional Organization of Theatres South, 1993.

Leviton, Richard. "The Holographic Body." *East/West Journal*, August 1988.

"Living Down Expectations," *Training Magazine*, July 1998.

Lovins, Amory. *Fast Company Magazine*, September 1998.

McCarthy, Kimberly Ann. "Creativity and Quantum Physics: A New Worldview Unifying Current Theories of Creativity and Pointing Toward New Research Methodologies." Diss. University of Oregon, 1990.

Milton, John. Sonnet XIX. *Complete Poems and Major Prose.* Edited by Merritt Y. Hughes. Indianapolis, IN: Odessy Press, 1957.

Nacchio, Joseph. *Fast Company Magazine.* June 1999.

Nachmanovitch, Stephen. *FreePlay: The Power of Improvisation in Life and the Arts.* Los Angeles: Tarcher, 1990.

Osborne, W. S. *Fast Company Magazine.* July/August 1999.

Perry, Tekla. "Managed Chaos Allows More Creativity." *Research-Technology Management,* 38, no.5.

Ray, Michael, and Rochelle Myers. *Creativity in Business.* New York: Doubleday, 1986.

Remen, Rachel Naomi. *Embracing Our Essence.* Deerfield Beach, Florida: Health Communications Inc., 1995.

Rich, Addrienne. *On Lies, Secrets and Silence.* New York: Norton, 1976.

Rilke, Rainer Marie. *Letters to a Young Poet.* Translated by M. D. Herter Norton. New York: W.W. Norton, 1934.

Robinson, Alan G., and Sam Stern. *Corporate Creativity: How Innovation and Improvement Actually Happen.* San Francisco: Berrett-Koehler, 1997.

Salk, Jonas. *Anatomy of Reality.* New York: Columbia University Press, 1983.

Schulz, Mona Lisa, M.D., Ph.D. *Awakening Intuition.* New York, Harmony Books, 1998.

Swartz, Jeffery B. *Fast Company Magazine.* July/August 1999.

Senge, Peter. *Cornerstones of the Learning Organization.* [Video]. New York and Washington, DC: Public Broadcasting Service, 1993.

Sheerer, Robin. *No More Blue Mondays.* Palo Alto, CA: Davies Black, 1999.

Sittenfeld, Curtis. *Fast Company Magazine*, issue 19.

Stratford, Sherman. "Leaders Learn to Heed the Voice Within." *Fortune*, August 22, 1994.

Swimme, Brian. *The Universe Is a Green Dragon.* Santa Fe, NM: Bear & Co, 1984.

Thiagarajan, Sivasailam. "A Playful Approach to Creativity Training." Seminar presented in Minneapolis, MN: American Creativity Association, April 26, 1996.

von Oech, Roger. *A Whack on the Side of the Head.* New York: Warner Books, 1983.

Wallas, Graham. *The Art of Thought.* New York: Harcourt, Brace and World, 1926.

Walton, Mary. *The Deming Management Method.* New York: Pedigree, 1986.

Wheatley, Margaret. *Leadership and the New Science.* San Francisco: Berrett-Koehler, 1994.

Wheatley, Margaret, and Myron Kellner-Rogers. *A Simpler Way.* San Francisco: Berrett-Koehler, 1996.

Yogi, Maharishi Mahesh. *On the Bhagavad-Gita: A New Translation.* Baltimore: Penguin, 1969.

Zemke, Ron. "Don't Fix That Company," *Training.* June 1999.

About the Author

Pamela Meyer is an educator, entrepreneur, artist, author, and speaker. As president of Meyer Creativity Associates, Inc., she works with organizations that want innovative solutions and teams that need to jump-start creative collaboration. In addition to her consulting practice and learning events, Meyer is a popular instructor at DePaul University in Chicago.

For more information on Pamela Meyer's corporate creativity programs or for interactive resources to spark your creativity, visit:

www.quantumcreativity.com

E-mail: pamela@meyercreativity.com

Pamela Meyer
Meyer Creativity Associates, Inc.
3540 North Southport, P# 405
Chicago, IL 60657

Toll-free (within the United States) (877) Yes-And-1
(773) 281-1901

Quantum Creativity is a trademark of Meyer Creativity Associates, Inc.